Role Playing in Psychotherapy

Role Playing in Psychotherapy

Raymond J. Corsini

Routledge
Taylor & Francis Group
LONDON AND NEW YORK

First published 1966 by Transaction Publishers

Published 2017 by Routledge
2 Park Square, Milton Park, Abingdon, Oxon OX14 4RN
711 Third Avenue, New York, NY 10017, USA

First issued in hardback 2017

Routledge is an imprint of the Taylor & Francis Group, an informa business

Library of Congress Catalog Number: 2010031145

Library of Congress Cataloging-in-Publication Data

Corsini, Raymond J.
Role playing in psychotherapy / Raymond J. Corsini.
p. ; cm.
Originally published: Roleplaying in psychotherapy. Chicago : Aldine, c1966, in series: Modern applications of psychology.
Includes bibliographical references and index.
ISBN 978-0-202-36393-6 (alk. paper)
1. Role playing--Therapeutic use. 2. Psychotherapy. I. Corsini, Raymond J. Roleplaying in psychotherapy. II. Title.
[DNLM: 1. Role Playing. WM 430.5.P8]

RC489.P7.C67 2010
616.89'1523--dc22

2010031145

ISBN 13: 978-1-138-53208-3 (hbk)
ISBN 13: 978-0-202-36393-6 (pbk)

« *To* DR. BINA ROSENBERG, *friend and colleague* »

Foreword

ROLEPLAYING IS THE most naturalistic of all the forms of psychotherapy. In the safety and privacy of an office, psychiatrists and psychologists can guide patients in more competent ways of living, helping patients to see in action how they behave. It is so easy for us to see what others do to us; so difficult for us to see what we do to others. Roleplaying, which can also be used for diagnostic purposes by the therapist, is an unparalleled procedure for letting the patient see himself in action, and helps him establish and assimilate in concrete fashion the insights he gets in the interview.

For many years I have championed the use of roleplaying and have employed it in my own office practice, mostly to supplement interviews, to help unfreeze patients from old, useless, habitual patterns, and to give them experience in new ways of acting. Properly used, roleplaying is a most valuable adjunct for therapists of any persuasion.

Raymond Corsini, a former student and colleague of mine, is singularly capable of this exposition. A clear and penetrating writer, he has provided psychotherapists with a most useful and practical manual covering everything that the experienced therapist needs to know about the therapeutic use of roleplaying. The abstracts done by Samuel Cardone cover most of the significant writings in this field and should give the reader a comprehensive understanding of the ramifications of the use of roleplaying. For the person involved in changing the thinking and values of others, this is a necessary book. No one has a monopoly on truth; no one knows all the answers. We, in the helping professions, must always keep learning about our theories and our practices. *Roleplaying in Psychotherapy* is a seminal contribution to psychotherapy, and I recommend it to all.

RUDOLF DREIKURS, M.D., *Alfred Adler Institute,* Chicago

Preface

ROLEPLAYING AS A psychotherapeutic technique is not as well understood as it deserves to be. The beliefs that roleplaying is an exotic method which commits the user to a special school of thought, that it is used only in group therapy, or that it is difficult to learn, are common erroneous notions.

This book is intended to give a clear picture of therapeutic roleplaying, and to explain how it is used and for what purposes. A rationale for its value and examples of its use are provided.

To supplement the writer's idiosyncratic presentation of roleplaying, Samuel Cardone has reviewed the significant literature of the field and has prepared a comprehensive annotated bibliography.

Many people have contributed to my understanding of therapeutic roleplaying. First of all, of course, is Dr. J. L. Moreno, whose genius is responsible not only for therapeutic roleplaying, but for the present status of group psychotherapy, and for a whole school of social measurements known as sociometry. As his student at Beacon, New York, the cradle of the sociometric-psychodramatic movement, and as an auxiliary ego with him on the therapeutic stage, I expanded my understanding of the uses and purposes of roleplaying. Among others who deserve mention in terms of what I have learned from them are, in order of temporal sequence, Dr. Rudolf Lassner, who introduced me to roleplaying while we were both staff psychologists at the prison at San Quentin; Dr. Lewis Yablonsky, whose technique as a psychodramatist is perhaps second only to Dr. Moreno's; Dr. George R. Bach, who has impressed me with his imaginative use of this technique; Dr. Wallace Lonergan, a student who outstripped his teacher; and Miss A. Ancelin-Schutzenberger, who was most kind in sharing her unique viewpoints and procedures.

Dr. William O'Brien, who has read the manuscript and made many valuable suggestions, and Dr. Bina Rosenberg, who urged the writer to complete a manuscript started many years ago, deserve the writer's and the reader's appreciation. I am also thankful to Mrs. Elinor Brown who read and improved the manuscript.

In the hope that the typical reader does not skip prefaces, may I paraphrase Dante and say: *Abandon preconceptions ye who read this book.*

RAYMOND J. CORSINI, PH.D.

A Note on Terminology

THE TERM ROLEPLAYING has four connotations: 1. theatrical, wherein players, following a script, simulate reality for the purpose of entertainment; 2. sociological, or patterns of behavior as dictated by social norms; 3. dissimulative, or deceptive behavior in which one tries to fool others by acting in a manner contrary to real intentions, emotions, or motivations; and 4. educational, whereby people act out imaginary situations for purposes directed to self-understanding, improvement of skills, analyses of behavior, or to demonstrate to others how one operates or how one should operate.

When used in psychotherapy, roleplaying falls in the last category. Essentially, it is a procedure for 1. diagnosing and understanding a person by watching him act out in a spontaneous manner a near-veridical situation; 2. demonstrating to a person or a group of persons how one should act; and 3. giving a person a veridical experience through having him play himself in various dramatic situations. This last aspect, a person roleplaying himself, is known as psychodrama—a word which is often used as the generic term for therapeutic roleplaying.

Contents

Roleplaying in Psychotherapy

« CHAPTER ONE »

An Overview

PSYCHOTHERAPY IS A learning process which can occur autonomously as in self-therapy, in a dyadic relationship between patient and therapist, or in a group situation with a therapist and six to twelve patients.

What is to be learned varies from patient to patient. Each person may present myriad interacting problems, symptoms, and complaints, but for the purpose of classification all problems can be separated into two major categories: (1) subjective states of discomfort such as feelings of inferiority, shyness, anxieties, guilts, tensions, and (2) behavioral insufficiencies or maladjustments, such as social ineptitude, withdrawals, rage states, inadequate functioning in school, on the job, in the family, etc. The patient expects that through psychotherapy he will learn to adjust better to himself, reduce his various internal, private conflicts and tensions, and thus arrive at a state of comfort and serenity; and also that he will become more competent in his overt life functioning.

From the point of view of the patient, psychotherapy has two main facets: *the personality of the therapist*—the kind of person he seems (to the patient) to be, the degree of interest he shows, his attitude toward the patient, his understanding and his wisdom; and *the procedures used by the therapist*—how he conducts the therapy, his systematic approach to solving problems.

The therapist sees psychotherapy as a process which helps the patient to understand himself, to come to peace with himself, to realign his thinking, to modify his attitudes and levels of aspiration, to accept himself, to learn new values, and new ways of behaving. It is a process of change in the sense of abandoning old concepts, coming to new generalizations, and learning new behavior patterns.

While therapists generally accept the same general aims of treatment, namely, improving subjective comfort and objective functioning, they differ in a variety of ways. First, each therapist has some sort of map of the patient, a prior conception of how he developed, how he learns, how he unlearns, what is the most desired state. This map is known as personality theory. Therapists belong to any of a variety of "schools" of personality theory, of which there are currently some two dozen major systems, each formulated to various degrees of completeness.[1] Other therapists, labeled eclectics, have no official connection with nor do they give a blanket acceptance of any single school of thought, but have developed their own systems, sometimes taking parts from two or more schools.

Whatever the map of the unknown that a therapist has, he operates in some manner consistent with his frame of reference but responsive to the nature of the person he deals with and to the nature of this person's problem. His method of operating may be called his technique. There are probably a dozen or so major techniques used in individual therapy, and twice as many in group psychotherapy. The purpose of this book is to discuss one class of techniques known as roleplaying.

[1] Hall, C. S., and Lindzey, G. *Theories of Personality.* New York: John Wiley and Sons, Inc., 1957.

« STRATEGY »

Strategy refers to the way the therapist approaches the patient. Speaking very generally, therapists may take a supportive position or they may take an uncovering or analytic position. In the first case, they want to comfort and reassure the patient; in the second case they tend to dig deeply into history and motivations. Another important distinction depends on the role that psychotherapists tend to assume in the relationship.

Some therapists see themselves as teachers. Why, they ask, would anyone want to come to us unless to take advantage of our training and experience? It is our function to diagnose the patient's personality and life situation, to explain his thinking, his feelings and his behavior, and to advise, counsel, and direct him. Therapists who assume this systematic posture are known generally as directive.

Other therapists see themselves as facilitators. They view the therapy process as essentially autochthonous, the therapist serving as a catalyst. Therapy, they say, is the exclusive function of the patient, a unique, personal, ineffable process which must be learned by the patient on his own. Therapists who assume this systematic posture are generally called non-directive.

Another important distinguishing characteristic is the road that therapists take to their goals. We can identify three major approaches: (1) Some therapists assume that the most appropriate medium is the intellect. Therapy is seen as a cognitive process, and so one listens and understands and then one advises, counsels, questions, interprets. The battleground is reason. The weapon is logic. (2) Other therapists believe the major approach should be made through the feelings. A person cannot be reasoned with, cannot unfreeze his attitudes and viewpoints unless he achieves an emotional state of relaxation and self-acceptance. Consequently, the therapist must encourage the patient through showing him acceptance. (3) Still other therapists approach therapy through action methods. They believe that the patient's thinking and feelings are relatively inaccessible but that behavior can be modified easily and, if modified, internal benefits will accrue.

The reader must not assume that with respect to supportive and analytic therapies, with respect to directive or nondirective approaches, or with respect to intellectual, emotional, or behavioral methods that any therapist can be precisely classified, or that he will always work consistently. Therapy is generally too fluid and too changeable a situation to permit rigidity, even though some therapists do tend to remain fairly consistent from session to session or from patient to patient.

« TECHNIQUES OF PSYCHOTHERAPY »

What do therapists actually do in relation to their patients and in terms of their various aims? What do they either suggest or permit their patients to do?

Questioning. Some psychotherapists concentrate on asking questions which can be subdivided into three groups: (1) Questions intended to elicit historical material, such as: "Tell me about your children." "What were your parents like?" "What are your earliest memories?" "What did you say then?" (2) Question intended to probe for thinking or feeling, such as "Why do you think so?" "Why did you feel this way?" "How do you usually interpret such behavior?" (3) Questions intended to challenge the person, such as "Do you think another person would react in the same manner?" "Suppose you do fail, what then?" "Would it be so bad if he does not care for you?"

Interpreting. A second common tactic is for the therapist to do the thinking for the patient and to explain to him the meaning of his thoughts, feelings, or behavior. Thus a therapist may say, "It seems to me that your earliest recollection indicates that you expect people to give you service." Or he may say, "Most likely your dream means that you feel alone in the world," or "Your behavior quite possibly may be seen by most people as selfish."

Advising. Therapists may assume the role of a wise man and, on an intervention continuum suggest ways of thinking, feeling, or acting. These may range from gentle suggestions such as "Don't you feel that this attitude—that unless you are the best you are no good—is really quite foolish?" through warnings such as "Unless you stop this behavior immediately you will get into serious trouble," to direct orders, "I want you to go into a restaurant and force yourself to order a meal, and I don't care about your feelings."

Narrating. Other therapists encourage the patient to talk a great deal. Both the technique of free association which Freud emphasized and Rogers's technique of reflection are likely to get the patient to do a great deal of talking.

There are many other techniques: confrontation, hypnosis, finger painting, music production, etc., used by therapists, but those discussed above are the major ones.

« ROLEPLAYING »

Roleplaying can be viewed as a technique which can be associated with every one of the procedures discussed above. It can be employed by therapists in the individual or group situation, and can even be used in self-therapy. Roleplaying, since it is only a technique, can be used by any therapist regardless of his theoretical orientation, and it has been employed by psychoanalysts (10, 115, 121 *), by Adlerians (88, 109, 111), by Rogerians (36, 43), as well as by eclectics (3, 5, 22, 59).

* Numbers in parentheses refer to the Annotated Bibliography following the last chapter.

Roleplaying can be used as a major technique or it can be used as an auxiliary procedure, supplementing other methods. It can be employed in a directive or in a non-directive manner. The therapist can use roleplaying for three primary purposes:

1. As a means of diagnosis. As the patient roleplays, the therapist may learn more about the nature and extent of the problem, how the patient actually operates, how he thinks and feels.

2. As a means of instruction. As the patient watches others roleplay, he learns how others operate in various situations.

3. As a means of training. Through engaging in roleplay, the patient may obtain insight into himself, may be able to learn to control his feelings or to develop new life skills.

DEFINITION OF ROLEPLAYING

Essentially, roleplaying is a "make believe" process. In therapy, the patient (and if it is to be an interactional situation, the others involved) will act for a limited time "as if" the acted-out situation were real. Some examples should help to clarify this definition.

Autonomous, subjective roleplaying. Let us consider a patient who is thinking as follows:

> Now this is what will happen. I will go into my boss's office and I'll say: "Mr. Smith, I have something to say to you," and he will say, "What is it?" I'll say "I have been with the firm two years." Then he'll reply, "Why do you tell me this?" and I'll answer, "Do you know how many pay raises I've gotten in that time?" and he'll say . . . .

Autonomous, behavioral roleplaying. Let us consider a person who is anticipating making a speech. In the privacy of his room he stands up and says:

> And now I wish to present our distinguished speaker of the

evening, Dr. Charlen. (He sits down, gets on his feet again, bows to the "audience" and says) Thank you, Mr. Chairman, and thank you ladies and gentlemen for your kind reception. As I face you I am reminded of a little story which may be new to some of you . . . (And so he rehearses his speech.)

Dyadic, therapeutic roleplaying. A patient is with his therapist and is talking.

P: I just can't get along with my wife. She is so unreasonable. She will argue about everything, and I'm just fed up with her. This morning, for example, she started a quarrel at breakfast.

T: What happened?

P: She wanted to know when I'd come home and when I told her I didn't know she got angry. For no reason at all.

T: Let's roleplay the breakfast scene.

P: What's that? Roleplay? I don't understand.

T: It's simple. I'll take the role of your wife. You play your own role. Let's repeat what happened. You try to act just as you did and I'll try to act as she does.

P: But you don't know my wife.

T: If I don't act her role properly, let me know and I'll try to imitate her.

P: O.K.

T: Let's make out my desk is the breakfast table. What's the set up?

P: She sits in front of me. We usually have juice, eggs, coffee, and toast.

T: She has prepared breakfast?

P: Yes.

T: What happens?

P: I get called to breakfast and I go out and get the newspaper, come to the table, and I read and eat.

T: She talks to you while you're reading?

P: Yes.

T: Fine. Here I am. I'm your wife and there's a paper. I'll call you, you pick up the paper and then you come to the table and make believe you're eating while you read. Do everything just as you did this morning.

T(W):* Breakfast is ready.

P(P): Let me get the paper. (He picks up the paper, comes to the table, lays the paper out, and begins to read it while going through the motions of eating.)

T(W): What time will you be home tonight?

P(P): Huh?

T(W): I said, what time will you be home tonight?

P(P): I heard you. I don't know.

T(W): I only want to know when to have supper ready.

P(P): I told you I don't know. Stop nagging me. You're always on my back!

T: Well, that wasn't too bad. Did I portray your wife accurately?

P: Pretty good. She nags me.

T: How about your behavior?

P: Normal.

T: Do you think that the way you responded was normal?

P: Well, maybe. She doesn't like me to read at breakfast, but I don't have much time otherwise. Maybe I ought to stop it. I can read my paper at the office. Maybe I did jump on her too fast.

This short excerpt demonstrates how roleplaying was used to supplement the interview which preceded and followed the roleplaying. The therapist suggested this situation to enable him to understand the patient better, and to permit the patient to understand himself better. The scene afforded a more real-

* The first symbol represents the roleplayer: the second symbol (in parenthesis) represents the role played. Thus T(W) means the therapist, T, plays the role of the wife (W). P(P) means the patient plays himself.

istic picture of what actually happened, evinced the nature of the husband-wife interaction, and made possible the classification of the patient's behavior.

It has already been pointed out that the various leading therapeutic systems tend to concentrate on one of the three major dimensions of behavior. As examples: Ellis's rational therapy [2] emphasizes logic and reason, the cognitive functions; Rogers's client-centered therapy [3] emphasizes emotions and feelings, the affective functions; and Slavson's activity group therapy [4] emphasizes acting out and interaction, the overt behavioral functions.

But roleplaying involves all three of these functions at the same time. In acting out a problem one acts, and feels, and thinks at the same instant. Moreover, this occurs in reaction to social stimuli which approximate normal stimuli in the individual's usual life situation. The structure and the circumstances of the acted-out situation tend to emphasize and exaggerate responses, so that frequently the individual is beside himself—gets angry, annoyed, upset, and behaves in a relatively ego-involved manner representative of his normal behavior. He tends to lose control because of the dramatic nature of the situation.

Consequently, one may postulate that roleplaying:

—Is a close representation of real life behavior.

—Involves the individual holistically.

—Presents observers with a picture of how the patient operates in real life situations.

—Because it is dramatic, focuses attention on the problem.

[2] Ellis, A. *Reason and Emotion in Psychotherapy*. New York: Lyle Stuart, 1962.

[3] Rogers, C. R. *Client-Centered Therapy*. Boston: Houghton-Mifflin Company, 1951.

[4] Slavson, S. R. *An Introduction to Group Therapy*. New York: Commonwealth Fund, 1943.

—Permits the individual to see himself while in action in a neutral situation.

THE SWIMMING ANALOGY

Let us return to first principles. Therapy is a learning process. The subject to be learned is how to live: how to behave, how to think and how to feel. One is learning a very complicated subject made more difficult by the tenacious hold most people maintain over the immutability and consistency of their own personality.

How do people learn similar complex activities best? A good example is swimming. What are the best ways of learning to swim? One could: (1) conceivably attempt to teach a person how to swim by cognitive means: letting one read books, view films, watch others swim, listen to lectures, etc., until the student knows everything about swimming, so that he could literally write a book on the topic and become an authority; or (2), one could assume that anyone can swim, since it is a relatively simple process, but what is needed is to remove a person's fears. And so we encourage the patient, let him express his fears, and get him to the point where he is not afraid of the water; or (3), we can let the person go in the water and practice, during which time he simultaneously learns the facts about swimming, overcomes his anxieties, and gets experience in making the proper motions.

Suppose we obtained three comparable samples of people, and gave each group the same number of hours in one of these three modes of instruction, and then threw them all into the water to see how many could make it back to shore. What percent, from each of the modes of training, could successfully meet this life test? Undoubtedly, the natural, holistic method would be the best.

The argument to be maintained and defended throughout this book is simply this: Roleplaying is a natural method of learning and unlearning various reactions to complex life problems. For this reason roleplaying can be effective for solving certain kinds of problems. It seems to have some logical inherent advantages over other methods of psychotherapy since it simultaneously attacks modes of thinking, feeling, and behavior—the entire province of psychotherapy.

« CHAPTER TWO »

Roleplaying Theory

WHILE ROLEPLAYING is only a technique, the person who wants to use it should understand what contributes to its unique advantages. No therapist can employ this procedure on an intuitive basis with satisfaction, any more than he could use the Rorschach technique without proper understanding and training.

« THE STRUCTURE OF ROLEPLAYING »

The unique value of roleplaying depends chiefly on three characteristics: simultaneity, spontaneity and veridicality.

SIMULTANEITY

We have already discussed the element of simultaneity in roleplaying in the swimming analogy. It is defined as the occurrence at the same time of several events.

Whenever we do anything, all dimensions of experience are simultaneously involved to some extent. If the behavioral act is of an emergency nature, crucial to the individual, every element is heightened. We act, feel, and think simultaneously in real life behavior.

This is perhaps the major theoretical advantage of roleplaying in therapy. The patient operates holistically, not partially. In a directive interview situation ("What do you think the reason could be that you feel upset when . . .") thinking, reasoning, analysis, problem-solving occur; the intellectual dimension is foremost. In a non-directive interview ("You sometimes get upset when . . .") sympathy, empathy, kindness, consideration are involved; emotional factors predominate. In activity therapy, such as art therapy ("Why don't you just smear the paint on the paper?"), the patient is primarily involved in activity; behavior is foremost.

In roleplaying, not only do these three elements of thinking, feeling, and acting occur at the same time, but, due to the summating effect of each on the other, they tend to be heightened—exaggerated—forced to fuller limits. The whole becomes more than the sum of its parts. The simultaneity of thinking, feeling, and acting tends to create total involvement. The person acts as a fully functioning totality because of the simultaneous functioning of these three dimensions, each reinforcing the other.

SPONTANEITY

A second important concurrent element has to do with the individual's creativity. Spontaneity is defined as natural, rapid, unforced, self-generated behavior to new situations. A person in complex behavior begins to wonder "What will happen if . . . ?" in relation to what he is doing. This thought is spontaneous, and is, in a sense, a creation. A lower organism probably would not wonder or make predictions. If a person's spontaneous reaction is appropriate and good, he has learned something "on his own." He learns in the process of reacting.

People are frequently placed in new situations: someone asks a question unexpectedly, something suddenly does not work. In such cases there may be no preplanned or previously learned specific responses. The person has to improvise, to do something, to react. To the degree that his response to the situation is good, i.e., satisfying, to that degree, his spontaneous or creative response helps him adjust and tends to become part of his repertoire.

A patient has trouble, he informs us, in dealing with his employer, in whose presence he feels tongue-tied, embarrassed, inadequate. This happens every time he meets his boss and each time he becomes more and more discouraged, the more so because he realizes, after the meeting, what he should have said.

The situation is acted out, perhaps in the therapist's office. Now, the patient may function well; he may respond appropriately to the contrived situation. Both he and the observers may feel satisfied with his performance.

He has responded creatively, since his *now* adequate behavior is new for him in such circumstances. But of greater importance, while he is behaving adequately in the situation, he is learning generalizations. He may be getting insights into why he functions as he does with his boss; why he feels so inadequate. He may suddenly stop the action and blurt out, "It is just like when I was with my father. My boss—my father, they both . . ."

And now, the therapist may match him in spontaneity and ask: "Can you recall an instance with your father that was similar to the one with your employer?" The patient does, and in a matter of minutes, a new roleplaying scene is possible. The patient plays himself, someone plays his father, and a new scene is acted. And, during this scene, as the patient acts, and thinks, and feels, he is learning—remembering, analyzing, comparing, understanding. In the process of roleplaying he is creating.

Frequently, after a "bad" performance, in which the patient roleplays in an inadequate manner, he asks to repeat the scene, or the therapist asks him to do it over. The repetition of the scene is usually superior. This is because the spontaneity factors occurring during the first enactment led to new insights and new skills. The therapist may call for a third performance, perhaps telling the patient, "Try to play it again, just as you did the first time." The patient now burlesques his first inadequate performance. Or, the therapist may, perhaps after discussion, ask the patient to repeat the situation, striving for higher levels of performance each time.

It can be seen now that the essence of spontaneity is the learning-while-doing in a situation devoid of threat.

But why not act thus in real life? Why does one need roleplaying? There are several possible answers to this question.

1. It is probably best to practice new approaches in real life. This is the best way to learn. But, reality situations can be too threatening, and the patient may not attempt new ways in real life. It would be best if a shy boy *would* get the courage to ask a girl for a date, but if he does not have the courage, he just won't ask.

2. Another reason is that if one fails in a reality situation the results can be harmful. Thus, if the shy boy does ask for a date and if he is turned down, he may feel so defeated that he will not try again. But, in therapeutic roleplaying one cannot fail. The very fact that the person has the courage to demonstrate his functioning, no matter how inadequately, is a "success." Consequently, in a therapeutic siuation, one is not embarrassed by poor performance. After all, that is why one is there; to show how one usually functions, and to be helped. The only "failure" would be refusal to try.

VERIDICALITY

The last of the three factors, veridicality, refers to the subjective reality of roleplaying.

In learning to fly an airplane by instruments, pilots enter an apparatus which simulates the cockpit of an airplane, so much so that were a pilot put in one while asleep, on awakening he might think he were at the controls of a real plane. He would hear the "motors" running, see the "stars" and the "moon" above, feel the trembling and the pitching of the "plane," and view the dials moving. While this apparatus is actually safely on the ground, perhaps in the basement of a building, nevertheless it has veridicality because it has verisimilitude. It seems real to the pilot.

Roleplaying can become a psychologically realistic experience. The person acting on the roleplaying stage is doing something similar to what he does in real life. A woman patient tells that she has frequent quarrels with her husband at breakfast. A "husband" is provided. The breakfast scene is recreated. A table is used. If possible, cups, saucers, silverware are put on the table. A newspaper is at hand, a radio may be turned on. All possible props are employed to generate verisimilitude which leads to veridicality

The "husband" is instructed what to say, how to react. Catch phrases are to be used. The patient may be asked first to play the role of her husband so that the "husband" will get cues about how to behave.

Does roleplaying become a realistic situation? Is it only playacting or is it a vital, meaningful, moving experience?

There is no single answer, since everything "depends." Some scenes fall flat. The main player does not catch on; the assistants do not meet his needs; the therapist cannot save the situation. In other cases, everyone catches fire. The air is electric . . . emotions are displayed . . . there is a sense of vital excitement . . . and one is struck by the miracle of birth, as the player and the assistants are transported into a world of their own; as the patient breaks through the chains that have bound him; as he releases himself in an instantaneous peak experience from the dead hand of the past, and emerges a new person.

Only those who have actually experienced such events can fully understand the almost unbearable excitement of the therapeutic instant in roleplaying.

Consequently, roleplaying cannot only become real, it can

become the most real moment of a person's life. The patient may break through his artificial façade and come to a "meeting" with another that transports him from his usual reality to a new dimension of meaning.

« INTEGRATION OF FACTORS »

In roleplaying the patient is engaged in a meaningful situation, interacting with therapeutic assistants who take roles in his private world, and he acts, thinks, and feels at the same time in his spontaneous responses to what they say and do.

What he is doing is meaningful to him, because he operates holistically, because he responds to new situations as they arise, and because the scene is realistic. If the purpose is diagnosis, others get to see him as he actually functions in reality; if the purpose is instructional, the patient in the audience responds with empathy because this is his life he is seeing; and if the purpose is training, he is almost painfully aware of what he is doing and how he is feeling, and what he is thinking; and in the process of roleplaying he is learning.

AN ILLUSTRATIVE CASE

A case in illustration of these principles may be provided. Al, a patient in a group therapy, tells the following story.

As a youth he went to work for his father, an umbrella manufacturer. He worked under his father's direction for thirty years. Two years ago his father retired and left the business to Al. Recently, however, the father returned, took up residence in his son's house, and resumed his place in the business.

The father is described as autocratic, dictatorial, unreasonable, rigid, demanding, impatient, violent, and explosive. When angry, he rants and raves working himself up into a fury. Retirement has not changed him a bit. Although somewhat feeble now, and burdened with a bad heart, he is the same curmudgeon he has always been. Al is desperate because his father's business judgment is not as good as it once was and he does not understand new problems. Al sees his father's behavior as leading to the possible destruction of the business. Trained to obey his father and to respect him, Al states that he does not know how to deal with him.

As Al told his problem to the group, and as he spoke of perhaps quitting the business and going somewhere else or even of trying to institutionalize his father, every member of the group realized the seriousness of the problem. Al explained that he had discussed the matter with his wife, business associates, friends, and relatives, but no one had come up with a good answer to his problem.

The therapist decided, for diagnostic purposes, to dramatize the situation. Al selected Bob, a member of the group, to take the role of his father. The scene to be acted was one in which the father was to upbraid the son for not doing something which the father demanded.

The scene took place, and within two minutes, Al, who had seemed to be a normally self-confident man, was backed to the wall, pale with fright as "Father" screamed at him. It was a most uncomfortable scene to watch.

Suddenly, while "Father" was shouting, Al ran out of the therapy room! "Father" was left speechless and all those present were puzzled by Al's headlong flight out of the room. An uneasy silence followed. Then Al appeared again, got on the stage and dramatically announced, "I have the solution. Now, I know what to do. Let's repeat the scene."

The scene was again played and as soon as the father began to scream, Al again ran out of the therapy room! Again, puzzled silence, and once again Al appeared, smiling broadly, and went on the stage.

"This time I'll play my father and you play me. As soon as

I start yelling, please run-fast-out of the room." The players switched roles and when "Father" (played by Al) began to scream, the "son" ran out of the room.

The hero of the drama turned triumphantly to the group. "That's the answer. Instead of just taking his crap, I'll run away and not come back until I'm calmed down. And if he starts again, I'll run again . . . and again."

This turned out to be a good solution. At the next session, Al told the therapeutic group that he had informed his father of what he would do, and then actually put his plan into execution. One day he ran away five times, once leaving the factory. Another time, while he and his father were talking with two important customers, he ran out of his office, and into a rainy street. Several times he had run out of his apartment. He assured his father he would even run out of the bathtub naked if necessary. Whenever his father would yell at him, Al would just run away.

Three weeks after the roleplaying session Al announced with the greatest satisfaction that his father had completely stopped his former behavior, and that other members of the firm, and even Al's wife and children had begun to run away from his father. The group roared with laughter at this revelation.

Sometime later he stated that his father had quieted down and that life was now much more peaceful. He also stated, and this is an important point, that he had learned that he had been inviting attacks, not only by his father, but by others by his pusilanimous behavior, and now had more courage and could stand up to people in other situations.

Let us analyze this case example of psychodramatic roleplaying in terms of the various factors involved. Al was at the same time thinking, feeling, and acting in the original roleplaying scene. This simultaneity led to the scene's veridicality, especially since his antagonist, Bob, did have a temperament like Al's father. While in this situation, and unable to respond to "Father" by yelling back, Al spontaneously got the idea of running away. When he came back, he not only was in command of himself, but took over the situation, again demonstrating spontaneity. Also, he told us that he experienced the delightful emotion of thwarting his father. When he came back the second time and took on his father's role, he had, as he told us later, the experience of knowing how his father would feel when Al would run away. Al defeated his father by running away from his domination.

His experience on the stage was a rehearsal of what he actually did later. By keeping to his self-generated solution, he was able to force his father to change his behavior. So successful, indeed, was this technique that others in the father's and son's social sphere began to imitate Al by running away. After about three weeks of this "insane" treatment the baffled and defeated father simply stopped his bullying behavior.

GENERALIZATIONS

Were a roleplaying session to be of specific value only for a specific problem, it would hardly be worthwhile as a psychotherapeutic technique. One would then need to have as many roleplaying experiences as problems.

The fact seems to be—and this is, of course, not unique to therapeutic roleplaying—that the lessons learned in a single session may not only be applied to a great many other similar situations, but much more important, the whole thinking, feeling, and behavior of the person may change in all possible directions as the result of a single session.

Al's success in dealing with his father, after what had been a lifetime of failure to do so, made him revise his estimate of himself in almost every dimension. Perhaps, surprisingly, a kind of reversal of relationships later occurred. With a new way of dealing with his father, Al's attitude toward him became more favorable. He saw his father as weak rather than as strong; an insecure man who had employed shouting to cover up his own anxieties and fears. Al actually became fonder of his father, more protective; and the father, too, became happier. All these beneficial changes seemed to depend on the instant when Al spontaneously got and acted on the idea of running; something he might never have been able to do in real life. He gained insight about himself and his father. He got courage. He learned a skill. Thus, he improved intellectually, emotionally, and behaviorally.

« THE DYNAMICS OF PERSONALITY CHANGE »

It is well known that personality is resistant to change, yet changes do occur, and if they did not (as the result of the combined efforts of patient and therapist), there would be little point to psychotherapy. Our purpose in this section is to point out why personality change occurs as a result of roleplaying; to attempt some explanation of the major dynamics of the technique.

Personality may be conceived of as a set of consistent expectations about oneself and others. These expectations add up to what sociologists call role-taking; that is to say, the role one assumes. This role is a fiction in the sense that it is assumed and not real, i.e., developed and not given. But the role one assumes in life must have some consistency, i.e., there is some kind of superordinate conception of self which enables the individual to function harmoniously and predictably. This is expressed by such statements as "Just like him to do that!" or "It's entirely in character," or "That's the kind of person he is."

Whatever the fundamental organizing nature of this superordinate directing principle, the name given to it is not important, but let us, for the moment, call it self-concept. There is a dynamic interdependent relation between how one acts and this super-principle, so that usually if one's self-concept changes, behavior changes. But what happens to the self-concept if it is the behavior that changes? Suppose one does something entirely out of character? What effect does this event have on self-concept? The event out of character is either "explained away" or else it is incorporated and becomes a new element in the self-concept, which now in turn affects all behavior.

A short but dramatic example of roleplaying illustrates this principle. In a therapy group in a training school for maladjusted and delinquent boys, one of the boys, George, speaks up as follows:

"Everybody picks on me because I'm a little kid. They just see me and they know they can hit me because I'm too small to fight back. If I did try to defend myself they would beat me up even more."

Poor George was not more than five feet tall and weighed less than one hundred pounds. The others in the group admitted that what George said was a fact; most kids did push George around.

The therapist then suggested an experiment.

"Suppose, George, we make out that you are King Kong; just a big hunk of muscle, all powerful, and no one could stand up to you, and you could beat up anyone you wanted. How would you like that?" George seemed shocked, but soon he said, "I'd like that." The therapist then asked the group members whether they could all play at being in absolute terror, to view the puny George as a monster, and to let him do whatever he wanted for ten whole minutes without any retaliation at all. Everyone agreed. Time was called, and George stood up, looked about, seemed ill at ease, and pointed to one member who shrank back. George moved toward him, and this person ran shrieking to a corner. George waved his hands menacingly at the rest of the group who shrank from him. He hit one person who fell to the floor, screaming in "pain." The others looked alarmed. George began to rain blows on the others, who crawled on the floor, huddled up, crying. In a few minutes George was in a rage, having driven every member of the group into corners and along the walls, yelling invectives and pummeling. When the ten minutes were up, the therapist was in a corner of the room, seated on the floor, protecting himself with hands and feet from the kicks that George was administering. When time was called, George was almost in hysterics.

The scene ended and the group went on to other things. At the next week's session, the therapist was surprised to see George's face almost literally black and blue, two black eyes, adhesive bandages here and there on face, arms, and legs. But George came into the room smiling through his bandages. Asked what had happened, he said the following.

"When I got out of this room last week, some guy pushed me. A guy who always did that to me. I hit him. He hit me back. I got up and began to fight him. He was hitting and hurting me. but I was enjoying it."

"But before you were always afraid of getting hit."

"I enjoyed it. No one can really hurt me. Inside I am King Kong."

"What happened?"

"Other boys stopped the fight. They said to him: 'What are you hitting a little kid for?' But I said: 'I'll beat that no good bastard. Let me fight him.' But they wouldn't let me. They said, 'George sure has guts!' "

"What else?"

"Anybody who touched me or hit me got a fight. I'm not

scared of anybody. I'm. King Kong inside." George went on to say that he had had about a dozen fights and "I made up my mind they have to kill me before I give up."

In subsequent weeks George had no more fights. He finally expressed his sentiments as follows.

"When you think you're weak, they pick on you. Now that they know I am not going to take any crap from anybody they leave me alone."

Independent observers, his cottage parents, his teachers, his social worker, all, when interviewed, stated that they had noticed favorable changes in George. He was more outgoing, cooperative, and generally better behaved. All of them commented, though, that for a time they couldn't understand George's belligerence.

George had taken a consistent role in life: the weak, scared, puny kid. And he demonstrated this to others by his behavior: his slinking walk, looking over his shoulder, eyes filled with terror, apparent fear, weak voice. His outward behavior was a consistent stimulus which provoked others to hit him. When they responded in this way, they confirmed his self-concept as puny, weak, and scared. One might conceive of the phenomenological structure as a kind of Gestalt, in which all elements of behavior led to an emergent: his basic self-concept; and this self-concept in turn determined his behavior. A neat, reciprocating stable self-system had been established which was reinforced by outside events, namely, how others treated him.

But his assumption in the therapy group of a role, though it lasted only ten minutes, that was contradictory to his self-concept, must have so shaken his self-concept that it changed into the notion: I don't have to be afraid of others. It didn't matter that what actually occurred in the therapy room was only play-acting. It was a veridical experience for George who grasped a new concept of himself, and changed the structure of all his thinking and behaving as a result of this one concept. He became aggressive, not so much because he had been successfully aggressive in the group but rather because his capacity to act in brand new ways and to succeed (though artificially) gave him new visions of how life could be different.

Change one element and you change the whole, is the essence of this idea. It expresses in the most simple manner the basic concept that underlies therapeutic roleplaying. Let a person get even a glimpse of the truth, a tiny portion of success, and if this is really incorporated into one's self-system, a change occurs.

This explains also why Al, who ran away from his father, felt in that moment that he was powerful, and that he could handle his father. Note that George fought and went toward people and that Al ran away and did not fight. Yet both forms of behavior resulted in superior adjustment *and* a better self-concept. The word "and" is really superfluous since behavior and self-concept are the two sides of the same coin: one, the external, the other, the internal, faces of the individual.

The skeptical reader may wonder at the apparent speed of change in both instances. It should be kept in mind that in almost all cases, personality changes in psychotherapy are of a saltatory nature. In therapy, one does not keep getting better a little at a time. Successful therapy usually consists of a series of discrete jumps, of sudden changes. In any form of therapy, patients, when they do change, tend to do so in readily identifiable steps rather than in imperceptible degrees. A sudden insight leads often to radical and far-reaching changes in all departments of life because the central structure is changed—a new self-concept has developed.

Roleplaying tends to be rapid in its effects because of the simultaneous functioning of the whole integrated organism in a realistic setting which permits the individual to employ his spontaneity. Poor little George as he kicked and struck those in the group was living life to the fullest: expressing his hatred, acting out his deepest daydreams, and meanwhile all this activity crystallized into the thought: This is what I am really like; this is how people really are; this is how I can be. When this realization sank in, there was a new George: proud, secure, tough, determined, and serious.

Real life situations can also make people change rapidly. A child who finds out that he is adopted; a boy who learns that a girl he admires loves him; a student who gets one-hundred percent on an examination paper; a soldier who performs an heroic act—any such event can, under the right circumstances, change an individual's self-concept.

« DYNAMICS OF ROLE THERAPY »

Psychotherapy can be conceptualized in terms of processes or in terms of functions. We could say "Psychotherapy is a procedure in which a person in a protected environment is able to discuss with a therapist his deepest problems. The therapist listens to the patient, analyzes his remarks, comments, behavior, and dreams, and gives him interpretations and suggestions." Or, we could define our topic in this manner. "Psychotherapy is a formal procedure in which a patient and a therapist attempt to achieve a sense of comfort and a higher level of functioning on the part of the patient."

One of the problems that the reader may have is that he may accept the first kind of definition as *the* definition of psychotherapy. If so, then he must assume that while roleplaying can be a useful adjunct to therapy, it is not therapy itself. In a sense, this is correct. Neither the interview, nor free association, nor hypnosis is the therapy. And neither is roleplaying. Therapy depends on the interaction between the patient and the therapist, on inner processes in the patient, and on the patient's behavior.

The final desired result of therapy, the inner comfort and the outer competence, can be obtained via passive-introspective methods and through active-behavioral methods of psychotherapy.

It is natural for therapists who have used the passive methods exclusively to come to feel that these are the proper procedures, and that activity in psychotherapy is an undesirable acting out, and thus an escape. But this is a prejudice, based on theoretical preconceptions and not on facts. We need only look at informal psychotherapy for examples. People are continuously "treating" themselves, dealing with their minor and major problems. In some cases people are able to deal with hostilities, jealousies, guilts, tensions, and other subjective anxieties by self-generated contemplative methods—by ruminations, prayers, meditation, puzzling out, self-analysis of motives, etc. Or, if the problem has to do with behavior difficulties, the individual may be able to think out his problem, convince himself that he can act in a proper fashion, and resolve to act in a satisfactory manner. In such cases, a patient does therapy on himself in an essentially passive analytic manner.

But other individuals obtain more or less the same results by actional techniques. Instead of lengthy ruminations, they act. A person who is afraid of facing his supervisor, goes out of his way to meet him. A husband who has been having difficulties with his wife brings her flowers and takes her out for dinner. A child who is afraid of the water goes to the beach to overcome his fear.

Now, the behavior directed to the problem tends to make the person more competent and more comfortable. That is to say that just as one can work out his problems in his head, and thus attain peace and competence, so too another person can attain both results simply by facing and dealing with that which is producing his fear.

The difference between approaches may be this: in an analytic intellectual type of therapy the patient may "understand" better the causes of his problems, while in action methods the patient may not get this depth of understanding. Whether such insights are really worthwhile is a highly debatable matter. However, when roleplaying is used, the tendency is for a person to gain insight *after* the superior behavior, and not before. One acts out a problem situation, handles it well, and *then* begins to understand the dynamics, purposes, and implications.

Consequently, roleplaying is not just some kind of conditioning training. One does not just learn new behavior without understanding. Behavior changes are accompanied by emotional and intellectual changes.

« THERAPEUTIC APPROACHES »

In directing learning, there are two general approaches. In one version, one first learns principles and then applies these principles to situations. Traditionally, for example, in studying law one is presented with general legal rules and then one studies cases which conform to the rules. This approach from the "top down" is known as the deductive method. That is, one learns the principle first, then applies it to individual cases. The other approach, known as the inductive method, calls for the individual first to deal with cases, and then come to principles.

Psychotherapists usually employ both forms of learning. An example of both procedures for the same problem is given by the following illustration. Let us say that a patient has mentioned that he thinks that people do not like him. Therapists D and I demonstrate a deductive and an inductive method of handling the patient, P, after having received the same information.

D: So you think people do not like you?

P: I am sure of that.

D: You are a constant stimulus, are you not?

P: What do you mean?

D: Others may differ, but you are the same. That is, they all see you. If they tend to have a common negative response to you, then it must be something about you that they don't like.

P: I suppose so.

D: Well, then, if we can find out what they don't like, and if you are interested in changing, then perhaps you can change and improve. Is that not so?

P: Yes.

D: Well, on the basis of what I know about human nature, and on the basis of my observations about you, I think I can tell you what people like in others, and what it is in you that they don't like.

P: Well, that is just what I want to know. Tell me, so that I can change.

D: People like people who like them.

P: I like people. I don't think I dislike . . . that is, I do like people and I want them to like me.

D: You say that you like people, but the problem is whether people think you like them. That is, do you demonstrate to them that you like them?

P: I think I do.

D: But what you think and what they think must vary. The issue now is this and the principle is valid—if you show that you like people, people respond favorably. If you show lack of interest, selfishness, unconcern, etc., then the people respond accordingly. If you can accept this as a general rule, then we can go ahead and examine individual instances of your behavior, to see whether your actions conform to this principle. In other words, how do you behave with others? Can you give me an instance?

P: Yes. Last Sunday I was at a party and I tried to tell a joke and nobody laughed.

D: Why do you think they did not laugh?

We see from the above excerpt that the therapist thinks he knows the answer before the discussion and he looks for specific instances to validate his hypothesis. He works from the general to the specific—the so-called deductive method.

And now for the same problem with therapist *I* who will use the inductive method.

I: So you think people do not like you?

P: I am sure of that.

I: Can you give me an example?

P: I told a joke a couple of days ago at a party and nobody laughed.

I: Why do you think they did not laugh?

P: I don't know. Maybe I didn't tell it well.

I: Under what circumstances did it occur?

P: They were talking about something else and I was reminded of this joke.

I: Do you think that your coming in with a joke at that time was appropriate?

P: I don't know.

I: Perhaps you told an inappropriate joke or told it at an inappropriate time.

P: Possibly. Now, there is this girl I like and she doesn't like me. I don't know what she has against me. Perhaps because I tend to tease her. And the people at the office. They think I am a know-it-all.

I: And how do they come to these conclusions about you?

P: I suppose . . . my behavior.

I: Something you do that they do not like. What could it be?

P: I don't know.

I: Is there anything that is general in these cases—the joke, the girl, the people in your office?

P: I suppose there is, but I can't see it.

I: Well, try to put yourself in others' places; what they think of you when you are operating.

P: Well, maybe . . . maybe they think I am a wise guy, trying to make an impression, trying to take over, not giving them any consideration. I suppose I just push my way, and make them feel bad.

I: Sort of like you aren't really interested in them?

P: They could feel that way. I am not too interested in them, but I want them to pay attention to me.

I: It seems then that you are asserting a general principle which underlies some of your social behavior. When you operate in ways that show lack of consideration for others, they will not like you.

P: Well, that's true, isn't it? And, I suppose that my behavior will strike them that way. I'll have to change my behavior so that I will not give that impression.

These two illustrations of how the same problem can be handled from the deductive approach and the inductive approach are given since, in general, those who use roleplaying in psychotherapy tend to employ the inductive approach. While this approach is not necessarily essential to the use of roleplaying, in general, this principle is maintained by roleplaying directors, who say, in effect, "Well, let us see how it goes and let us try things out and see what comes out of specific cases."

That is, the therapist who may think he knows what is wrong, still gives the patient a chance to learn by himself through a process of replaying a particular act. Instead of dealing with vague generalities, he concentrates, and even magnifies a problem, hoping that the patient or that others who see the patient in operation will come to useful generalizations. An illustration of this occurred in the case of a man who was having trouble in his new job as a supervisor. He had no idea why he was not succeeding. For the purpose of diagnosing the problem, the therapist suggested that he roleplay a particular situation. On the basis of his roleplaying behavior, it became clear to all why he was having difficulty. He did not permit others to have their say; he interrupted them continuously. This was an example of his general behavior and led to the conclusion that he wanted his own way at any cost and did not really respect the opinions, wishes, or feelings of others. This general conclusion was inferred from small bits of behavior demonstrated to the group.

Just as the diagnosis of the problem was made from actual behavior as shown in roleplaying, so too the treatment of the problem was in terms of small bits of behavior. This man was asked to listen to tape recordings of himself and to contrast his verbal behavior with that of others in similar situations. He now was forced, on the basis of the evidence, to conclude that he did interrupt continuously. And then, once he had accepted the validity of the judgment of the diagnostic group, he was asked to replay the situation over and over again until he was able to listen patiently to those who were playing the role of subordinates.

However, only when he understood the difference between what he had been doing and what he was now doing, when he was able to make verbal generalizations, such as "People do not like those who interrupt them," was it felt that he had made real gains, and that he would be able to transfer his new behavior in these particular situations to other situations.

This case illustrates the difference between the two approaches. The "from the top down" therapists tend to deal with deductive principles ("Everybody has inferiority feelings" or "One's behavior is a function of interaction between instincts and conventions"), and look for illustrations to support their views. The "from the bottom up" therapists look for specific unit behaviors and come to generalizations on the basis of examples. Deductive therapists tend to deal with big problems (values, motivations, attitudes, developmental factors, etc.), and attempt to direct the patient in terms of theoretical conclusions. Inductive therapists tend to be less theory-centered, to operate in terms of here-and-now, common sense approaches, and concern themselves with relatively small elements of behavior, hoping that by making changes in unit behavior elements, generalizations will result.

Both the inductive or the case-centered approach and the deductive or general principles approach aim at the same result—better behavior and greater understanding. The inductive approach sees the behavior change as coming first with the generalizations following. First one acts properly and then one comes to understand the principles. In the deductive approach, first one comes to have better understanding, and then proper behavior follows.

While roleplaying does not necessarily depend on the inductive approach, generally roleplayers tend to be more pragmatic, less theoretically centered. They tend to work with specific situations and to come to conclusions after, rather than before, the roleplaying.

« SUMMARY »

The three major theoretical elements that contribute to roleplaying's effectiveness as a therapeutic technique are simultaneity, spontaneity, and veridicality, or the simultaneous existence of heightened thinking, feeling, and acting, in contrived but realistic situations in which people are forced to find new and appropriate solutions. These three principles often cut through resistance and lead to rapid beneficial change and increased understanding.

Roleplaying is generally based on the inductive principle; one learns complex matters best from unit behaviors which lead to generalizations. The therapist operates in such a manner as to magnify small situations to the point that the individual comes to conclusions either on his own or with the help of others. This is in contrast to the general position that some therapists take who have prejudged a situation and then try to find examples to illustrate the general principles.

The effects of roleplaying, and of other forms of therapy, are *central* (new ideas, new understandings, insights about self and others, more courage, more comfort with self, relief of anxiety, etc.), and *peripheral* (new skills, new habit patterns, new ways of dealing with others, etc.). Both the central and the peripheral are aspects of the same thing: peripheral behavior is the analogue, the outward manifestation of central self- and other-concepts.

« CHAPTER THREE »

The Process of Therapeutic Roleplaying

AS IN OTHER forms of psychotherapy, privacy is required. The ideal room is one in which the members will feel comfortable and safe; in which there are no extremes of light or noise and where there will be no interruptions. The usual office of a therapist is sufficient, especially if there is some room to move about. If roleplaying is done in a group, the best arrangement is a circle or a semi-circle. Members should sit close to one another.

Recording devices can be helpful, but only if the recordings are clear. In some cases a room must be carpeted or soft hangings must be set up; otherwise playback will be harsh and unpleasant. If the recording machine has an odometer type of counter which will permit a specific "spot" to be located for playback, this will be quite helpful. Theoretically, a talking movie would be an ideal instrument for psychotherapy. Kagan, Krathwohl, and Miller [1] report making video tape recordings of psychotherapy sessions and playing each session back immediately to the patient and therapist. By such procedures, both the therapist and the patient can see their behavior as others see it.

[1] Kagan, N., Krathwohl, D. R., and Miller, R., Simulated Recall in Therapy Using Video Tape: A Case Study. *Journal of Counseling Psychology,* 1963, 10, 237-243.

« PREPARATION FOR ROLEPLAYING »

The therapist must be honest with his patient or patients. If roleplaying is a new experience for him he should say so. He should present it as another therapeutic procedure.

We shall give examples of how one can present roleplaying for the first time in individual and group situations. Let us say that Mr. Adams is in psychotherapy.

INDIVIDUAL THERAPY

T*: Well, now, Mr. Adams. You state that Mr. Brown, your supervisor, has it in for you. Talk to me as though you were he and as though I were you.

A: I don't understand. I don't know what you mean.

T: He said something to you.

A: Yes, like I said. He said, "Where are the figures?" and I told him . . .

T: No. That's not what I am asking for. I'll be you. You be him. Talk to me like he talked to you.

A: Why?

T: I want to get the feeling he generates. I want to learn for myself how he operates.

A: You want me to act him and you'll act me? I can't see the reason for it.

T: There's a good reason. Now, let us see. Were you at your desk?

A: Yes. He came to me . . .

T: Please stand up and come to me and act like your supervisor. Talk just as he does.

A: O.K.

* To repeat the notations: A stands for Adams, B for Brown, and T for the therapist. Adams playing Brown, the supervisor, is A(B); the therapist playing Adams is T(A).

A(B): Where are the reports?
T(A): What reports?

A: No. That's not what I said. I said, "I don't have them ready." And he . . .
T: O.K. Let's start all over. Come to my desk.

A(B): Say, Adams. Where are the reports you promised?
T(A): I don't have them ready.
A(B): What the hell am I going to do with you? What's wrong with you now?

T: That's enough. I think I understand. Now let's switch roles. You act yourself and I'll act Brown.

T(B): Say, Adams. Where are the reports you promised?
A(A): I don't have them ready.
T(B): What the hell's wrong with you anyway? What's the matter with you? What am I going to do with you?
A(A): I meant to do them.
T(B): I'm sure you did, but I need them now.
A(A): I'll get them to you when I get them finished.
T(B): And when will that be?

A: That's exactly what he said. And I said . . .
T: Please don't tell *me* what you said. Let's stick to your telling Brown.

T(B): When can I get those reports?
A(A): How do I know? Too many interruptions here. How can I work with these interruptions? I asked you to put me in another office, but you didn't. And now you want me to go out of my way for you. Just because you're the office manager doesn't mean you can push me around . . .

We have attempted here to have Adams object more, and interrupt more than usually occurs. Another example from individual therapy may give the flavor of a therapist initiating roleplaying.

Mrs. Parris states that she has great difficulty with her mother-in-law who calls her frequently on the telephone, keeping her for a long time. She does not know how to handle this situation. Let us listen to her as she expresses herself in the interview with the therapist.

"She seems almost to know when I am busy, like just when we are about to eat. And then she talks and talks and talks. I don't want to offend her and my husband would be hurt if I just hung up on her, but she really drives me wild."

The therapist says:

"I'd like to understand what goes on. Let us roleplay the situation. I'll turn my back to you and you turn your back to me so we can't see each other. You play the role of your mother-in-law and I'll play you. I'll try to act as I think you act and you act the way your mother-in-law acts."

The therapist and his patient now reenact the telephone situation. This gives the therapist information so that he can play the role of the mother-in-law.

"Fine. Now, let us change roles. I will now play your mother-in-law and you be yourself. Try to act on the phone just the way you usually do."

This time the therapist obtains a clearer idea of how his patient reacts to the mother-in-law.

After this scene, the therapist may talk with the patient, giving ideas about how the problem may be handled. Or, he may decide to use roleplaying for training. He might say:

"Let us do it again. You play the rôle of your mother-in-law again and I'll play you. But this time I'll talk differently; the way someone else might handle this situation."

So, they may go through the "telephone" conversation once again. This time the therapist, by behaving differently from the patient, is giving her information about how the situation might be handled.

After the third situation has been enacted, the conversation between them might go as follows:

"Well, Doctor, it makes sense how you did it. But I don't know if I could do it that way."

"Would you like to try? I'll act the way your mother-in-law does and you can try a different approach."

And so they roleplay once again and this time the patient attempts to vary her approach.

STARTING ROLEPLAYING IN GROUPS

From time to time, the group therapist can introduce a procedure to enhance what he may think needs further intensification. Roleplaying is a useful procedure for this purpose. One should wait until a natural situation arises for which roleplaying would clarify the discussion.

T: I wonder if it might not be advantageous to act out your problem, Bill.

B: What do you mean, Doctor?

T: Well, let us review what you have told us so far by actually seeing what happened. We know what you did but we don't know how you did it. If we set up a situation in which you show how you actually met the situation we may learn more about you. Are you willing?

B: Why not? How do we go about it?

T: Well, I'll need two assistants: a man to play your father and a woman to play your step-mother. Can you find someone here who you think would fit the roles?

B: Mike will do for my father and Francine might be able to handle my step-mother.

T: Fine. All right with you, Mike?

M: O.K. But I don't quite know . . .

T: I'll explain. Francine, will you play Bill's step-mother?

F: Why me?

T: Well, Bill. Why did you select Francine?

B: Well, Francine looks and acts something like my step-mother. But if you don't want to . . .

F: Oh, all right. What do I do?

T: Here's the set-up. Bill will first tell Mike a bit more about his father, and you, Mike can ask him questions; same for you, Francine. It is most important that Mike and Francine understand the kind of people Bill's parents are so that they can invest their roles with authority. The rest of the group should cooperate by watching quietly so as not to destroy the illusion we want to establish.

The above may be a typical start. There is usually no difficulty in working out arrangements. The therapist does well, however, to select problems, at least in the beginning, which will not be too complicated or offer too much difficulty, reserving tougher problems for later sessions.

There are many specific techniques in roleplaying which we shall elaborate later but a good beginning rule is simplicity. Simple straight roleplaying, handled well, can meet needs in most instances. More complex procedures will be used when the director of roleplaying gains more confidence and more skill.

« THE ROLE OF THE DIRECTOR »

Perhaps in no other form of psychotherapy does the therapist face so great a technical challenge as in directing roleplaying. A really significant session can be exhausting, and if it goes as the therapist wishes it to, he will have an exhilaration far beyond that which can occur in any of the quieter and more passive forms of psychotherapy.

The writer has met and watched in action, most of the outstanding roleplaying directors of today, and believes that they tend to have some temperamental and intellectual similarities which may account for their using roleplaying. Those roleplaying directors whom the writer has known appear generally to be creative, venturesome, and ascendant. Since one has a tendency to become what one does, directing roleplaying has an effect on the therapist as well as on the patient. Consequently it is likely that regardless of the director's original personality, continued working with this technique tends to change him.

CREATIVITY

The director who uses roleplaying must decide whether A's problem can be roleplayed successfully. Once he has made this decision, he has these creative tasks. What shall be the problem? Who should be in the scene? How should the problem be structured? Which format is best?

The director must depend not only on his own creativity; he must also be able to fit into the intended drama the ideas of others. He may have to subordinate some aspects, emphasize others. He decides where in the stream of life he begins the drama, who takes which roles, and how they are to emphasize them, and when to stop the action. Meanwhile, if the roleplaying is in a group, he must consider the effect of the scene on the patient, the assistants, and other members of the group.

While at times his problems in these respects are made

easy when the projected scene is readily structured and a relatively simple format is appropriate, there are times when his fantasy becomes a high form of art: he knows that the proper approach is unique and so unusual that no one else would ever think of it, and he knows that this approach will work.

Effective roleplaying calls then for creativity on the part of the therapist. It is not merely a matter of saying, "Well, should we roleplay?" It is a matter of creating a complete situation, fitting a format to it, or even inventing a new one; selecting personnel and delineating roles. All this must be done quickly. Conventional dramatists can take months to work out their plots. The roleplaying director must be able to do somewhat the same thing in the few minutes at his disposal. He improvises, but the improvisations must have structure and meaning. All must hang together and he must keep in mind the many elements—the needs of the hero of the drama, the needs of the other patients, etc.

VENTURESOMENESS

Roleplaying directors, at least as the writer sees them, tend as a group to be more unconventional, more ready to try new approaches, more available to new ideas than the general run of therapists. It is not enough to be creative to be a good director of roleplaying. The very nature of the process seems to call for a certain amount of courage in trying new procedures. One cannot hesitate too much in doing roleplaying. A certain amount of decisiveness is required as well as the capacity to take chances. The typical roleplaying director *seems* to know what he is doing. His assurance is based on his belief in himself—his readiness to experiment. Yet he must always be concerned with such issues as: Should he try this particular scene? Should he take a chance and put a great deal of stress on the patient? Might the anxiety generated be too much to handle? How might the others in the group react to the situation?

The venturesomeness of the good roleplaying director must not be confused with foolhardiness. Directing roleplaying involves a great deal of artistry and complicated decisions about what will work and what will not work. The director who would try anything lacks creativity. It is the combination of good judgment, insight into others, and ability to predict consequences of situations, which leads the good director to make decisions of quality. A psychotherapist without much courage, or with little faith in the ability of people to withstand the stresses of a really meaningful session would not be able to direct roleplaying in psychotherapy.

ASCENDANCY

Theoretically, one can be creative and courageous and still not be a good director. A third quality is required. For lack of a better term it may be called ascendancy. This refers to stage presence or, more accurately, to leadership quality or salesmanship. It is a charismatic quality.

A good director is firmly in command of the situation. He starts the action, directs the players, calls them on and off stage, and is able to control the group as an instrument of therapy. He is forceful and tactful, strong and tender, and varies his degree of control or domination in a manner appropriate to the situation.

In some cases, patients balk, others want to go their own way. Unless he is able to permit people to show their own originality, the director may stifle this creativity; on the other hand, chaos may result if things get out of hand.

The good roleplaying director runs the show. He is the authority but not the tyrant. He is dominating, but not domineering. His iron fist is concealed in a velvet glove. He is able to start and stop, facilitate and slow down, initiate and change, all in a smooth manner. These skills grow out of practice.

« THE THERAPIST IN ACTION »

Let us assume that we can know what goes on in a therapist's head as he conducts roleplaying. Here is an example of an interchange between the therapist, T, and his patient, Andy. The italicized material represents the therapist's thoughts.

A: I started heavy drinking in college. As a child I saw that my father, who was a successful lawyer, drank a lot, and I felt repelled by it. My mother was terribly upset by his drinking. I was a rather sickly child and when I went to high school, I was determined to become an athlete. I worked hard at athletics and did well. But when I went to college, I knew I couldn't compete and I felt rather inferior. Others seemed so much more capable than I. Well, I got into a fraternity and I soon found that when I drank I was able to relax more, and I guess this started it.

T: You felt more at ease with others when you drank. . . . *Probably over-ambitious, feelings of insecurity, imitation of a successful father and rebellion against a domineering, moralistic mother.*

A: What bothers me is that I always felt I could take or leave booze alone. I never was a solitary drinker. I thought that if I married I wouldn't need drink. Well I've been married three months and I've started again. Matter of fact, I'm drinking quite hard. That's why my wife sent me to see you.

T: I see. *He's come here reluctantly; probably does not want to change; bright fellow; was sick as a kid; probably is able to use helplessness, such as sickness or alcoholism as a weapon; have to learn more about him, but must approach this carefully.*

A: My wife is worried about me.

T: Yes. *Possibly his mother also worried about him when he was sick.*

A: I really don't want to upset her.

T: I'm sure you don't mean to. *Maybe that is just what you do want to do; dominate her by your weakness.*

A: So, I try to control myself, but it has been getting worse.

T: Andy, I'd like to try a bit of roleplaying. Just to clarify something. *Let me make it neutral, so as not to scare him.* I'd like to get a feeling of your parents. Did they discuss your father's drinking?

A: Oh, yes.

T: *How he emphasized the "Oh." I may be on the right track.* Well, let us make it simple. We'll have your mother and father talking about his drinking. One of us will take your father's role, the other will take your mother's role. Which one would you prefer? *Wonder who he'll select and what it will mean?*

A: Mother's, I guess.

T: *Mother? Why? Well, let's see.* O.K. Where are we? I'm Father.

A: Let's say that you've come home. You are a bit under the weather and I'm waiting up for you.

T: (Standing up.) Do I stumble. Is my speech affected?

A: No. Apparently you are in a good mood.

T: Well, let's begin. You start off.

A(M): John, where were you?

T(F): With the boys.

A(M): You didn't call me.

T(F): Couldn't get to a phone. You know how it is.

A(M): You've been drinking again. You know you shouldn't drink to success.

T: *To success? Sounds like an important slip of the tongue.*

T(F): Oh, I'm in control of myself. You know that.

A(M): Well, I don't like it.

T: That's enough. I get the feeling. Mother didn't really seem too upset. Your father was an attorney, was he not?

A: Yes. He was quite a good attorney; was quite successful.

T: Did he drink, as you do, in college?

A: No. He told me that he had been brought up to avoid alcohol, and I got the impression that he didn't begin drinking until after he started his law practice. His drinking never affected his judgment.

T: *Maybe, my friend, you equate his success with drinking and think this may be your talisman.* Do you think his drinking perhaps loosened him up and enabled him to actually do a better job?

A: I don't know. I'd hardly think so. But he did seem to be in a better mood with a couple of drinks. People liked him better, I think.

T: Perhaps he did make a better impression on others when he was relaxed. What effect does drink have on you?

A: It makes me tense at first, but after I have a lot I relax.

T: You need a great quantity? *He seems to equate success with drinking. How can I explore the possibility that in his private logic he thinks so?* Let us now try a roleplaying scene with your wife. I'll be you. You be your wife. *Let's see what comes out.*

A: Why should I play her part?

T: *Why this reaction?* So that I'll get a feel of her attitude and then I can play her if necessary. I'll bring in my receptionist to play your wife if you wish.

A: I don't think it necessary.

T: *Wonder why?* All right. Let us work it out together. Where are we?

A: I've come home and I have had too much to drink.

A(W): Where have you been?

T(A): Out.

A(W): You've been drinking again.

T(A): Just a little.

A(W): You know you can't handle drink. I just can't stand it. Why do you do this to me? You know you become helpless.

T(A): *Helpless? Looks like I was on the right track.* What do you mean by that? I can handle myself. I'm not drunk or anything.

A(W): Oh, darling, I feel so bad about it.

T: O.K. I get the picture. Let's reverse roles. This time I'll play your wife.

A: This is painful to me.

T: Good. Maybe we'll get somewhere. Please stand up; come in; act just as you usually do. *Looks like we're getting to him.*

A(A): Hi, Honey.

T(W): Andy! What's wrong with you?

A(A): Nothing. What the hell gives you the idea there's something wrong with me?

T(W): You promised.

A(A): I can handle myself all right. Don't start sniveling.

T(W): *Well, it's my clue to cry.* (Begins to cry.) Oh, I never thought things would come to this. Only married three months. (Sobs.)

A(A): (Gets on his knees before the therapist.) Stop it, Honey. You know I don't like it when you cry.

T(W): *Let me try this line.* I want you to be a success, and now . . . (Sobs.)

A(A): (Becomes visibly upset.) You're wrong. Drinking won't hurt me. I swear I have control. I drink because I like it. It doesn't harm me at all.

T: O.K. That'll do it. Let's discuss it now. *Seems like we're on the right track.*

A: Gosh, Doctor, what do you think? Am I becoming an alcoholic? Why do I drink?

T: Do you have any opinion?

A: You used my wife's very words. Like you knew her.

T: *Let's see how he reacts to this.* I suppose most wives don't like to see their husbands become failures via drink.

A: Do you think drink can hurt me, really?

T: What do you think?

A: I don't know. It didn't really harm my father. I felt pretty bad when I roleplayed. It was very real.

T: What do you feel like when you start drinking? . . .

This short example shows how the therapist thinks, and how he can use roleplaying for diagnosis, instruction, and training.

« THE ASSISTANTS »

In roleplaying, we define two roles: the hero, or the protagonist, and the assistant, or the auxiliary ego. The hero is the person on whom the session is focused. It is he who has the problem; he who wants to improve. The person who acts against him, be it the therapist, a nurse, or another patient is known as the assistant.

One might think that serving as an assistant is a matter of convenience only for the hero. If Sam has a problem with a colleague, and if Joe agrees to play the colleague, then one might think the experience will not be therapeutically valuable for Joe. Such, however, is not necessarily the case. The person who plays the role of assistant may be helped on his own path to improvement, due to altruism, empathy, and self-illumination, among other factors. The more roles one can assume or understand, the more likely one is to be socially competent.

ALTRUISM

The typical patient in therapy is wrapped up in himself. His perception is constricted. He is concerned with his self too much. Only *his* problems are important. He is self-centered.

But when a patient in group therapy helps another by becoming the assistant, when he comes into direct confrontation with another person with a problem, when he volunteers to help another person in distress, getting involved with the problems of another can be beneficial for him. For a while someone else's problems become real.

Usually, the therapist calls on the assistant to report on how he felt in this role, asks him to tell how he viewed the patient. This now puts the patient into another helping role. He becomes a quasi-therapist, assisting someone else in trouble. He shares with him. Let us listen to a dialogue between the therapist and the assistant immediately after a roleplaying scene with Mr. Jones.

T: Art, can you tell us how you felt as you interacted with Mr. Jones?

A: Yes. I felt Jones was unfair to me. He kept interrupting me. He didn't listen to my explanations. Whenever I'd try to get a word in edgewise, he'd cut me off. I began to get hostile. I felt like telling him off, but I tried to hold my temper, and I thought, "Well, this is how he must make his brother feel," and so I let go. I can see how Mr. Jones can upset people by his domineering ways.

EMPATHY

A second reason why the assistant gets value out of roleplaying is that he begins to understand the person he plays and the person he plays against. By putting himself in a strange role, by responding to a strange person, he begins to enlarge his inner world. Selfish, narcissistic people have trouble playing other roles. They are rigid and unyielding. Through assuming unusual roles, they develop their social sense and their empathy.

Thus, a young delinquent playing the role of a mother whose son is a delinquent, becomes able to understand mothers and to appreciate his own mother's feelings.

SELF-ILLUMINATION

The patient, in meeting another person on stage, may in effect confront himself. He sees the other taking positions with respect to life that he takes. This encounter can be almost traumatic in its effect. "Why, he acts just as I do!" an assistant may say. This notion that another person is like oneself is usually quite a revelation.

Still another aspect of the same area refers to the realization that even in a new role one operates on the basis of inadequate flexibility, that one cannot throw himself into another's role. "I just can't think like her," a patient may state, "somehow or other I keep answering from my point of view, not from hers."

INTEGRATION OF ASSISTANT FACTORS

The changeover from patient to assistant helps the therapist in his work because it keeps patients alert and interested, democratizes the situation, gives people opportunities to experience a variety of roles, and puts patients in a direct helping position. If the roleplaying occurs in individual therapy and if the therapist assumes the assistant role, he is able to feel the impact of the patient in a more meaningful manner. The therapeutic encounter is stronger.

« SUMMARY »

Roleplaying can be used in individual or in group psychotherapy. No special equipment is necessary, although the use of props to attain verisimilitude, and the use of recording equipment for playback can be useful. Roleplaying directors come in all sizes and shapes, but they generally appear to be creative, venturesome, and ascendant, which may be a function of what roleplaying does to them. Directing a session calls for the therapist to think quickly and to make many decisions, and so it is a highly active process. While the roleplaying is going on the therapist gets more information about the patient and this kind of acting out tends to lead to the emergence of new situations to be explored. If therapy is done in a group, participation in the roleplaying problem of any member benefits the others by getting them involved in helping others, by giving them better understanding of others, and by enabling them to gain insight about themselves.

While the roleplaying procedure is essentially simple, and can be compared to the interview, its range of potentialities is great and therapists can vary widely in their abilities to use it.

« CHAPTER FOUR »

Roleplaying Procedures

« FORMATS »

ROLEPLAYING directors have developed a considerable number of structured procedures for a variety of therapeutic purposes. J. L. Moreno has been especially inventive in this regard.

STRAIGHT ROLEPLAYING

Straight roleplaying or psychodrama has already been illustrated. This occurs when a person plays his own role against someone who plays another's role. Two major possibilities exist.

1. A(A) × B(B)
2. A(A) × C(B)

In the first case A and B play themselves. If they are a married couple demonstrating a typical incident of their lives, each is the hero. The second, however, is the more common form. A plays himself, while C, an assistant, plays the role of B.

In some scenes there are more than two players. Thus, if a husband and a wife play themselves and if their children are symbolized as C, D, and E, the structure might be as follows:

A(A) × B(B) × F(C) × G(D) × H(E).

In probably more than half of the roleplaying situations this straightforward format is used. When a number of scenes are employed, the first one usually is of this type. Succeeding scenes are suggested by straight roleplaying.

ROLE REVERSAL

The most popular format variation is known as role reversal. The A(A) × C(B) format now becomes A(B) × C(A). A, the hero of the drama plays B, his antagonist in real life, while C, the therapeutic assistant plays A. In this manner A both lives the role of his antagonist and is able to observe "himself" as played by C. Role reversal has two subvariations. In one case, first the situation A(A) × C(B) is worked out, and then it becomes A(B) × C(A). In the second case the action is interrupted at some point and the two people who are roleplaying switch in midstream, as it were. The two change roles and continue from the point of interruption.

An example may help to illustrate role reversal. Mrs. Allen, a patient who has a problem with her son, is interviewing Mr. Brown, a school principal, played by C.

A(A): But, Mr. Brown, don't you think my son can adjust to other children?

C(B): Possibly, Mrs. Allen, but you must change your attitude toward him.

A(A): I am a good mother. I don't know what I do that is wrong.

T: Change roles please; just switch and continue. (Roleplayers change chairs.)

C(A): But, Mr. Brown, I really try my best. I really do.

A(B): Mrs. Allen, I don't know whether you have or not.

C(A): What can I do? I really have tried everything that I know of.

A(B): I don't know what I can tell you to do.

T: Shift again. (Again, they shift chairs.)

C(B): You ask me what you should do? Well, has anyone told you what to do with your son?

Putting Mrs. Allen in Mr. Brown's role forces her to see herself from Brown's point of view. Role reversal helps the patient to see himself as others see him and also gives possibilities for empathizing with someone else. In the example, Mrs. Allen may be angry with Mr. Brown, but when she almost literally becomes him, she finds that she has to think as he does. She finds herself in his place, and consequently begins to appreciate his point of view. In playing his role, she is able to see herself as he sees her. This format can effectively awaken a person to social reality quickly and forcefully.

ALTER EGO FORMAT

This is a rather tricky procedure and calls for an experienced and sensitive assistant. A(A) $\times$ C(B) is the first situation, but then someone else enters the scene, D, who becomes B's alter ego (B′). D speaks what he imagines to be B's inner thoughts. An example may be pertinent, returning to the scene recently discussed.

A(A): But, Mr. Brown, can't you give me hope?

C(B): I'm afraid not, Mrs. Allen. We can only do our best. It is your problem now.

T: O.K., D, please be B's alter ego and express how he probably feels. (D goes behind B, out of sight of A, and when he talks he intends to let A understand the inner thoughts of B. A is not to respond to D(B′) but only to C(B).

A(A): I can't understand why you won't do anything. I need help.

C(B): Madam, I've explained my position very clearly. It is not our problem.

D(B′): *This woman will drive me out of my mind.*

A(A): Mr. Brown, I've thought it all over and I'm sure that if you could give James another chance . . .

D(B′): *What, again! This woman is impossible. How can I get her out of my office?*

C(B): I'm afraid not. This is all I can say. James must go.

D(B′): *Please go, please go, won't you? Do I have to throw you out?*

A(A): I am disappointed with you. James is really a good boy. I'll talk to him.

C(B): As I've said, it is impossible.

D(B′): *Don't you understand—IMPOSSIBLE!*

The director can employ the alter ego technique to give the hero insight about how others may be thinking and feeling. In a situation such as the one illustrated, the following discussion may occur following the playing of the scene.

T: Mrs. Allen, how did you react?

A: I'm sure that Mr. Brown does not feel at all the way D reacted.

T: Well, let us ask C who played Mr. Brown. Did D express your feelings?

C: Precisely. I was angry with Mrs. Allen. She was so persistent and just didn't seem to get my feelings at all.

A: You mean you felt I was too . . . aggressive?

C: I really didn't feel sorry for you. I felt sorry for James that you are his mother.

A: Oh!

T: What do you mean by that?

C: You are possessive, smothering, just the kind of neurotic woman who is almost a caricature of the over-protective mother.

A: That is not true. My relationship with James is very good.

T: What kind of a boy is James? . . .

The therapist may now develop another scene. Let us assume that it is played out by straight roleplaying and that now D becomes James's alter ego, D(J′). Here might be part of the scene.

A(A): Now, James, you just *must* improve. All I have done for you. What will ever happen to you?

B(J): Mother, I try my best. They don't give me a chance. They pick on me.

D(J′): *Actually, Mother, I enjoy making trouble because I know it upsets you.*

A(A): You know your behavior upsets me.

D(J′): *That's what I want.*

B(J): I'll try to behave better if I get a chance.

D(J′): *Like hell I will.*

It can be seen why the alter ego format is tricky. D, playing J′, may not actually be able to express James's inner feelings. But the fact that the person who is playing the alter ego may be completely wrong, does not necessarily invalidate the value of the scene in terms of the effect it may have on the mother. For example, in a post-roleplaying discussion, the following may occur.

A: Do you really think that my son can feel this way?

D: Well, I don't know. You are a kind of aggressive and overpowering mother figure. James may not be able to say what he feels to you.

B: I felt somewhat the same. There's such an intensity about you. I can't imagine your son standing up to you; and he may well want to get even.

T: Mrs. Allen, we are speculating about your son's feelings about you. It is possible that his behavior is directed at you; but it is also possible that he does not realize it. On the surface he may be grateful and loving, but there may be a deeper current of resentment.

A: People are complicated. You all seem in agreement that I'm a powerful person.

T,B,D: Yes.

A: Maybe so. My husband says that, too. Maybe I should just let James handle his own problems. Suppose we try to do it by roleplaying. I don't know if I can really do it.

T: Let's try the mirror technique, Mrs. Allen. First, we'll show you how you act; then, we'll try to work out the situation in a different way. B, will you play James again, and D, will you play Mrs. Allen as you see her?

MIRROR TECHNIQUE

We can now see how the same scene might look when played by [D(A) × B(J)] ←A. This symbolization means that Mrs. Allen looks on while D plays her role and B plays the role of her son James. We shall introduce still another variation. C will now become Mrs. Allen's alter ego, C(A′). He will attempt to express her feelings while she watches D play her role.

D(A): Well, James, we have to have a little talk.

B(J): What about, Mother?

D(A): Your behavior in school.

B(J): Oh, again?

D(A): Yes, again. I've made up my mind to change my behavior and my attitude toward you. You are fifteen and should know how to handle your own affairs.

C(A′): *Oh, I never could talk to James like that!*

B(J): What do you mean, Ma? You know they all pick on me.

D(A): Nonsense. If they do, they have a good reason. I've decided that you are at fault.

C(A′): *James at fault? How could I ever think that?*

B(J): Don't you love me, Mother? I don't understand why you are talking this way.

C(A′): *Of course, you don't. You are so used to me protecting you.*

D(A): You have to grow up, my son, and fight your own battles.

B(J): But I am growing up. You always told me that it was everybody else's fault.

D(A): I don't care whose fault it is. You stand on your feet and meet your problems. I am not going to see Mr. Brown. I am writing to him to do what he sees fit. If you want to stay in school, *you* should see him and you handle it.

B(J): But suppose they throw me out?

D(A): I'll be sorry for you and I'll do what I can but I think that if you apologize it will be better than if I intercede for you again.

C(A′): *It sounds good, but can I really talk to my baby in this manner?*

In this situation, Mrs. Allen watches someone else play her and listens to "herself" handling a problem in a different manner. Meanwhile C(A′) tries to verbalize what Mrs. Allen's inner thoughts might be. In this way, she is surrounded, as it were, by people who are putting pressure on her to change.

Following every scene, there may be extended discussion. Five minutes of roleplaying may call for a half hour of discussion. Let us now assume that Mrs. Allen is half-way convinced and that the therapist now decides to use still another technique.

DOUBLING

Mrs. Allen is asked to go on the stage and talk out loud to herself about her feelings in this matter. B now becomes her alter ego. The situation is that Mrs. Allen and B are on stage, back to back.

B(A′): *I'm just so confused.*
A(A): Yes, I am.
B(A′): *So much is going on. Can I really be that wrong?*
A(A): I am not so sure.
B(A′): *I am a good mother. Everybody tells me so.*
A(A): Yes, they do.
B(A′): *But here, in this roleplaying, they criticize me. Why?*
A(A): I suppose they mean well.
B(A′): *But what do they know? They have never even seen James. All this roleplaying. . . .*
A(A): Yes. I try my best. James is a difficult child.
B(A′): *Oh, what should I do?*
A(A): I feel sad. I try my best to be a good mother.
B(A′): *Yes and I don't really think I am not a good mother. I do try my best. But maybe I have made mistakes.*
A(A): We can all make mistakes.
B(A′): *So maybe I have made mistakes. Everyone can make mistakes.*
A(A): I can change if I want to. Yes, I could act this new way. I could say to James, "School is *your* problem." That's what I could say.
B(A′): *"It's your problem, James. It's up to you."*
A(A): "You have to handle your own problem. Don't come to me all the time. You're old enough to settle your problems. Don't always be expecting me to help you out."
B(A′): *But how will James act? How will he feel about me? Won't he think I am rejecting him. "Mother," he'll say . . .*
A(A): Yes, "Mother," he'll say, "don't you love me?"
B(A′): *My heart will break.*
A(A): I'll feel so bad. I want him to be my . . .
B(A′): *Baby!*
A(A): Yes, he's my baby. I don't want to lose my baby.

As can be seen, the double technique has some elements in common with the supportive, reflective, non-leading technique of Carl Rogers.[1]

OTHER VARIETIES OF FORMATS

The ingenuity of roleplaying directors is indicated by the fact that although we have listed several format variations here and in the glossary, many more have been used. Indeed, every roleplaying director invents new variations to meet the needs of special situations. It is much more important, however, for a director to learn how to use a limited number of techniques such as the ones described above than to have partial command of a great many. Once these basic formats are mastered, one can attempt some of the more complex ones.

« STRUCTURING ROLEPLAYING »

How does one know when to shift from questions and answers, or from narration, to roleplaying? This is a question of judgment but the therapist who comes to ask himself the question, "How does the patient actually behave?" has reached the point where he should consider employing roleplaying. Or, suppose there is an impasse and the therapist simply finds himself blocked with the patient's apparent obtuseness. Or, the therapist may believe that the cathartic effect of reenacting an unresolved problem may be valuable and so may suggest roleplaying. Or, the therapist may feel that the individual simply does not see himself, and so will roleplay to give the patient an understanding of how the therapist sees him. Or, perhaps the patient simply seems to need improvement in some skill and so the therapist may roleplay to help him develop competence.

[1] Rogers, C. R. *Counseling and Psychotherapy.* Boston: Houghton Mifflin Company, 1942.

In general, when a problem arises that cannot be handled by more conventional methods of the interview, interpretation, or narration, roleplaying can be considered. In many cases, the therapist has no idea what will happen. What actually occurs may be a surprise to him and give him an entirely different picture of the patient. Roleplaying may open up new areas for investigation. In some cases, a short drama, which seems to have no particular meaning, at least at first, stimulates the patient and tends to generate meaning.

A familiar situation is that in which a patient will not talk. The therapist is frustrated and perhaps is even annoyed by the reluctant patient. Such cases are relatively frequent with adolescents who are sent for therapy. Let us eavesdrop on one of these situations.

T: How are you today, Harold?

H: Fine.

T: How was school?

H: O.K.

T: Do you have anything you want to talk over with me?

H: I dunno.

T: What happened since I saw you last?

H: Nothing much.

T: Surely something happened.

H: I went to school.

T: What happened in school?

H: Just the same. The teacher talked.

T: About what?

H: The usual things. I don't listen much.

T: Do you know why?

H: I dunno.

T: Look, let us try to understand each other. I want to help you but you have to tell me what is on your mind, what you are thinking, what your problems are. Unless you cooperate, we'll get nowhere. Maybe that is what you want?

H: No.

Every therapist has run into such cases which tend to make life difficult indeed. These situations, while most common in referred adolescents, also occur in self-referred adults, who for one reason or another, are unable to produce sufficient material. Let us assume in the case of Harold that the therapist is getting impatient, and that he gets therapy moving in the following manner.

T: Have you ever heard of roleplaying?

H: No.

T: Let's have a little fun. I want to show you something. Are you ready to try it?

H: What is it?

T: Come here and take my seat. (Stands up.) Just sit here and let us pretend that you are me. (Patient takes the therapist's seat.) Now, I'll make out that I am you. You try to imitate me and I'll try to imitate you. Do you think you can imitate me?

H: Sure.

T: O.K. I'll go out of the office and then I'll come in and let us see who can imitate who best.

H: O.K.

(Therapist comes in and sits down in the chair that Harold usually sits in. He looks at the floor the way Harold usually does.)

H(T): How are you?

T(H): Fine.

H(T): What's your problem?

T(H): I dunno.

H(T): Why don't you know?

T(H): I dunno.

H(T): What's the matter with you anyway?

T(H): I dunno.

H(T): We ain't going to get anywhere this way. Don't you want to talk to me?

T(H): Yes.

H(T): Say something. This is costing your parents a lot of money.

T(H): Don't know what to say.

H(T): Why don't you know?

T(H): I dunno.

H(T): I think you're crazy.

T(H): Maybe.

H: (Breaking out of the roleplaying.) We ain't going to get anywhere this way.

T: (Also breaking out of the roleplaying.) I agree with you. What can we do?

H: I dunno.

T: I dunno, either.

H: I like sitting here.

T: O.K., you can keep that seat. Why do you like it?

H: Well, it is more important. I am always being talked to.

T: You'd like to be the boss?

H: Sure. Everybody is always telling me things. Why do I have to be always picked on?

The resourceful therapist might use other variations of roleplaying in meeting this or any other kind of impasse. The therapist's creativity is of the essence in using roleplaying procedures. He must use his judgment to decide when a particular format is probably suitable.

The question may arise about the degree of structuring necessary. How much preparation should there be before roleplaying is engaged in? This is another problem that requires judgment. If a patient has used roleplaying to some extent and so is sophisticated, it may be enough for the therapist to say: "Let us act out that problem. I'll take the role of your partner and you be yourself. We'll be in your office and I'll come in mad because you didn't keep your word and I am pretty sick about the whole thing." This may be enough instruction in some cases. In other cases, much more information is called for. An example may be appropriate. Let us assume that Mrs. Anthony is in group therapy and is narrating.

A: And like I said, my mother, my brother, and my sister-in-law get into the act and they take my husband's side. You'd think I was always to blame.

T: How did it go?

A: Like usual. I am the fall guy. I am the patsy. They all ganged up on me.

T: It might be worthwhile acting out this situation. You talk a lot about your family and maybe we ought to meet them. What is your husband like?

A: You mean who is he like in this group?

T: No. Describe him. What is he like?

A: He's very fat and he has a little beard. That beard drives me wild.

T: What kind of a person is he?

A: You'd think he never made a mistake in his life. He just can't see any other side to any issue except his own. He is just perfect, thank you.

T: Anything else?

A: Everything his sister says is right, everything I say is wrong. I can say it's hot when it is ninety-five degrees and she can say it's cold, and she's right—not me.

T: And your mother?

A: A nonentity. She always sides with the strongest one and it isn't me.

T: And your brother?

A: Another nonentity. He is just like my mother. No opinions of his own. He works for my husband and doesn't dare to have any opinions.

T: And the sister of your husband?

A: She's like him. You'd think she never had to go to the bathroom. Oh, no. They are all perfect on my husband's side.

T: And yourself?

A: I'm just trying to be myself. I am trying to stick up for myself. That's the problem.

T: Now, the situation had to do with your buying a car. How do they all fit into this situation?

A: My husband wants to get a new car. You know I had an accident with the old one. So, we make a big deal about what kind of car my husband and I are going to get.

T: But where do the others come in? What are their points of view?

A: My mother is putting up the money because my husband is short of money. My brother is an auto mechanic of sorts and he is supposed to be an expert. My husband's sister is a know-it-all and she sticks her nose in everything.

T: What car do you want to get?

A: A convertible. A Buick.

T: And what do the others want?

A: They all want to get a used Ford.

T: What argument does your mother give?

A: That I have too many accidents and shouldn't get a new car.

T: And your husband?

A: He needs the car for his work and he sometimes has valuable things in it and a sedan is safer than a convertible. But I tell him . . .

T: Not now. We can act it out. What is your husband's main argument?

A: The cost.

T: And your brother's argument?

A: Well, he knows this used car, and he says it is a very good buy for the money.

T: And your sister-in-law?

A: She has the craziest idea that I just want to show off that we have money.

T: Looks like we got a good part of the story and now let us see if we can get various people to act out the problem. Who can take the part of the husband?

Getting all this information is valuable in and of itself. The person being interviewed is giving information and possibly in answering the questions is beginning to see things in a new light. Certainly the members of the group are forming impressions and coming to have opinions. Let us assume now that the situation has been structured to this point and that various individuals in Mrs. Anthony's forthcoming psychodrama have now some understanding of the various personalities and the various points of view held. The situation is further structured as follows.

T: I think we all understand the situation fairly well. Ann Anthony wants to buy a Buick convertible. Her mother does not want to put up so much money, especially since she thinks that Ann is likely to have an accident. The husband believes that a sedan is more convenient for him. The brother knows of a sedan that is a good buy. The sister-in-law thinks that Ann wants the car to show off. Now, Ann, where did the scene take place?

A: In my living room.

T: Let us arrange the chairs in the same relation as they are in your living room. Will you tell us where to put them? (Chairs are adjusted.) Now, who sits where? (The various antagonists are placed in their proper places.) Now, who starts off the whole thing?

A: Anybody could.

T: Let us start off with you, then. Here is your family. You have all been discussing the car and you are going to make a final argument for yourself. O.K.?

A: O.K.

A(A): Like I said we need a good car and when I go out with the kids I want them to have a lot of fresh air, and I want a car with a lot of power because you sometimes get on those hilly roads and it just isn't safe not to be able to go fast.

B(Sister): But Ann, you can open the window of any car and get all the air you want. You know that isn't the reason you don't want a sedan.

A(A): How do you know?

C(Brother): Now, Annie, be a good sister and listen to me. This Ford has plenty of power. It is a V-8, and it will go up a hill just as fast as you want.

D(Mother): Besides I am not putting down four thousand dollars on a convertible. And they are not safe anyway. You'd think you'd think of your children, the way you drive.

A(A): Two accidents in one year and one was definitely not my fault. Big deal!

E(Husband): What did the insurance company say?

A(A): I'm always wrong in the eyes of my husband. It is always my fault.

E(Husband): All I asked was what did the insurance company say.

A(A): You know damn well what they said.

A scene such as the foregoing can be continued as long as the therapist believes it worthwhile. When he feels that enough material has been obtained for purposes of discussion, he may stop it and open the floor for comments. Let us see what might happen during the discussion period.

E: I got to say one thing, Ann. You are pretty aggressive. You want your own way and you just don't care what others think. I believe your sister-in-law was right and you'd admit it too if you were honest. You want a convertible just to make a show.

A: What if I do? Sure, I do. What's wrong with that?

E: Why didn't you admit it to her?

A: I will not. Give her the satisfaction? Not me!

B: It was obvious to me and I suppose to all your family that that was the reason you wanted the convertible. Perhaps you should have admitted it.

A: Then, would I get it?

B: Possibly not, but you're not going to get it anyway, and even if you do, you'll be so miserable that you won't be happy with it.

D: I hate to tell you this, Ann, but you have absolutely no idea how aggressive and unreasonable you are. You say your husband and his sister are aggressive and think they are never wrong, but my god, if they are any more aggressive than you are, I'd be surprised. Don't tell me you are just a little lamb.

A: Well, I got to defend myself, don't I?

And the therapy goes on. This was an illustration of straight roleplaying with perhaps the usual amount of structuring and preparation. The therapist might decide to repeat the situation with someone else taking Ann's role, and Ann in the "audience," so that she can see how she operates, etc. Or, after the roleplaying, the therapist might shift topics immediately, letting Ann come up again some other time, and hoping the reenactment will lead to greater understanding of how she operates.

A bit of further analysis of this situation may be worthwhile. We note that considerable interviewing took place prior to any roleplaying. In this manner, every member of the group begins to get a picture of Mrs. Anthony and also more or less an idea of the various people in Mrs. Anthony's world. This then enables them, when they assume the various roles, to get some idea of how they should act. Arranging chairs, etc., to resemble the real place where the group would meet helps to establish verisimilitude.

One must not conclude that because the problem apparently involves a trivial issue that the roleplaying effect may be trivial. The important issue appears to be Mrs. Anthony's relationship with other members of her family. Her negative view of her family members may soon be countered by negative views of the group members about her behavior. If the members of the group tend to say the same things about her that the real members of the family say to her, this information is likely to be very impressive, since it comes from neutral individuals. In this manner patients can "learn" what they already "know." To hear a certain message from a disinterested party may be much more meaningful than to hear the same message from a person close to oneself.

Part of the artistry in directing roleplaying has to do with shifting from straight interviewing to roleplaying and back again. How long the director continues his interviews, how long he permits group discussion to go on, what kind of roleplaying scene he establishes and how long he lets it go on, are all elements relating to his artistic use of roleplaying.

« SUMMARY »

In this chapter we have discussed a number of basic formats such as A(A) × C(B), or straight roleplaying in which an individual, A, plays himself, and C, a member of the therapy group, plays B, someone in A's life space. When A plays the role of B, this is an example of role reversal, characterized by A(B) × C(A). When the role reversal takes place during the action, and straight roleplaying changes, this is known as switching. In the alter ego format, a third person enters the situation. The alter ego now speaks out the hidden thoughts of one of the participants. In, for example, straight roleplaying, A(A) × C(B), we may have someone act as the alter ego of A, and we would symbolize this role as D(A′). The whole symbolization might be: A(A) × C(B) × D(A′). A fourth common format is the mirror technique in which the patient watches someone else play him. Thus, if A has played a scene, we may now ask D to show A how he acted, and we may have [D(A) × C(B)]←A. The double technique calls for someone else to think along with the patient. The format may be symbolized as follows: Ȧ(A) × B(A).

The resourceful therapist may find that these standard procedures do not meet his particular needs and he may use his creativity in developing new situations. The artistry of roleplaying lies in the proper use of formats, in knowing when to introduce them, how long they should last, and how much time to give to other procedures such as interviews and group discussions.

It is best to use roleplaying sparingly at first, to depend on simple formats, and in general to operate in a conservative manner.

With experience, the therapist who experiments with roleplaying will begin to get a feel for the procedure. Whether to employ roleplaying or not, which variation to use, how long to continue using it, how to direct discussion, etc., are necessarily matters of judgment, and the correct decision cannot be established in advance.

« CHAPTER FIVE »

Roleplaying in Diagnosis

A NUMBER of diagnostic procedures are used in clinics when time and resources are available. They often include a social history, physical and neurological examinations, objective and projective testing, and the interview. Diagnosis frequently occurs without much help from the patient, who, because of conscious attempts to deceive, minimize, or exaggerate, or who, because of various adjustment mechanisms, unwittingly gives inaccurate information.

A patient may say that he is "all right," "nothing bothers me," "I had a happy life," "I love my parents." And he may believe each statement and yet the diagnostician may conclude that the patient is disturbed, that he had a wretched life, and that he hates his parents.

A diagnostician would be most secure in his conclusions had he been able to see the patient during his childhood and formative years, and were he able to see him in action in normal social situations. On the basis of such observations he could formulate a much more accurate understanding of the patient. But this is usually impossible, even though one can obtain recollections of the patient from those who have known him. But the evidence of family and friends, teachers and employers, is frequently inaccurate and often consciously so, due to a desire to protect, minimize, or exaggerate, or at least to weight the evidence unfairly.

In some cases, roleplaying can supplement more traditional approaches by giving additional and sometimes crucial evidence about the causes and extent of a condition. An illustration will elucidate this point.

THE INTERVIEW

Therapist: What happens to you in a group?
Patient: People don't seem to like me.
Therapist: Do you do anything to upset people? What's your group behavior?
Patient: Just like anyone else's.
Therapist: How about when you get excited or emotional?
Patient: Like I said, like anyone else.

Roleplaying Illustration. This patient, P, and two assistants, Al and Bill, roleplay a social situation and a heated discussion takes place. Below is an excerpt.

Al: I don't know about that! I think there are two points of view.
P: Sure, the right one and yours!
Al: Well, I could be right, couldn't I?
P: In the pig's eye you could.
Bill: Let's see why Al thinks so.
Al: Once, I was in a class . . .
P: Where?
Al: What's the difference?
P: Trying to weasel out? I thought so. I just know you are making it up.

A scene of this kind would contradict the patient's statement that he is "just like anyone else" and would give the diagnostician a view of how the patient actually operates.

The reader may think that if a person is clever enough to

lie, claiming that he operates "just like anyone else," that he could then "act the role of just anyone" in roleplaying and subdue critical attitudes, loud voice, annoying mannerisms. Quite the opposite is true, for two reasons.

The first reason is that people often just do not see themselves; they are frequently unaware of how they behave and how they impress others. They are blind to themselves.

This generalization should be acceptable to any therapist and needs no particular elaboration. As a matter of fact, one of the most common effects of successful therapy is insight, or new and better understanding of oneself.

The second reason is that it is very difficult for a person to "fudge" a role in roleplaying. One tends to play oneself.

Putting an individual in a realistic situation in which he has to respond to questions, comments, and gestures quickly, surprising him with various unexpected situations (especially if he does not strongly wish to deceive), tends to lead the patient to fall into well-established patterns and he will begin to display his usual reactions. The self-consciousness involved in acting before a group tends to rattle the person and this causes him to regress to familiar ways of acting. In a short time, the person is so taken up in the situation that he forgets himself, forgets where he is, forgets that it is only a demonstration, begins to become involved, becomes oblivious of observers, and, as he warms up, begins to act in his usual manner.

Contradictory impressions can be made on observers by the patient in an interview and by the patient in roleplaying. The insistence of the roleplayer that he acted "just like anyone else" when it is quite clear to every observer that he acted in a socially inept manner leads to diagnostic insights.

The observer gets a sample of real life behavior via roleplaying due to the capacity of this procedure to simulate reality. In roleplaying we tend to act ourselves.

A CASE EXAMPLE OF DIAGNOSTIC ROLEPLAYING

A patient stated:

> "I asked my husband if he would let me have use of the car, and he said he could not because he had to have the car greased that day. I asked him if he couldn't have it greased some other day but he said, 'No.' I didn't argue with him and just went out of the room."

The patient was asked to roleplay the scene and after a two minute demonstration it was obvious that what she had said while sitting down, and what she had demonstrated on her feet were two quite different things.

In the dramatic exposition she approached her "husband" in a defiant manner, used a wheedling and yet demanding voice, and when her "husband" refused her request in a reasonable manner, she stamped her foot, turned about abruptly and walked away in evident anger.

In short, the two communications were quite different. Listening to this woman tell her story created one impression but watching and listening to her as she reenacted the scene created a very different impression.

Which of the two communications was truer to the facts? The patient was asked: Was her demonstration realistic? She said it was close to the truth. Would she like to see how she had behaved by having someone else reenact her part? She said she would.

Another woman in the group then replayed this short scene, trying to act in exactly the same manner as the original patient. After the scene was played, the therapist then asked the patient to comment on the accuracy of the portrayal.

> "Well, I don't think it was quite right. She (the other woman

who had played her part) seemed to be loud and angry. I was more quiet and controlled."

The therapist then asked the group this question: "Who seemed to be angrier and louder?" Unanimously the group agreed that the original patient had been louder and angrier than the second patient. The original patient protested that this could not be so and the matter rested there. At the following session she reported that she now accepted the group's version, that she had been watching herself and realized how angry and loud she really was, and that she had changed. In another replaying of the same scene she now reacted in a quieter and more reasonable manner.

This is an illustration of the value of roleplaying as a method of communication. It was evident that something was wrong in the patient's communication process. She told the group how she saw herself and her husband. Then the group observed her in action and came to a quite different conclusion. Finally, the patient came to accept another version of her own behavior as true. This in turn led to changes in her home behavior, which led to a better relationship with her husband.

While people may be keen observers of others, they may not have a true picture of their own behavior. They may present a gross disparity between communications and behavior and be unaware of the differences. They do not recognize themselves when they see themselves "as in a mirror" through roleplaying presentations. When the disparity is made evident, this may lead to "outsight" and people can change their ordinary behavior.

« ROLEPLAYING AS A PROJECTIVE TECHNIQUE »

Whenever a person roleplays he demonstrates his unique personality, giving others a diagnostic impression. Others can see how he responds to novel situations, can make estimates of his intelligence, his flexibility, his habitual modes of thinking, get impressions of attitudes, etc. Consequently, roleplaying can be used as a projective technique.

The writer has used the following situation as a roleplaying projective technique. A table and chair are provided and the subject gets these instructions.

> "This is a test. You are to listen carefully to the instructions but not to ask me any questions. We want to see how you react to these instructions. Is that clear? Listen carefully and ask no questions. You see a table and chair. On the table there is also an invisible book, an invisible candle, and an invisible pencil. The test will last precisely three minutes. You are to go to the table and chair and do or say whatever you want with the invisible book, candle, and pencil. Be as inventive as you can."

Now, how do people react? Here are some responses.

1. One type of patient begins to ask questions and will not budge unless such questions as "Why," "What's the purpose?" "Do I have to?" are answered. Or he makes remarks such as "No, I won't. It's silly." Perhaps one out of twenty responds in this manner or refuses to participate.
2. A patient goes to the table, sits at the chair, picks up the "book" and "reads" for the entire time.
3. A patient picks up the "book," "leafs" through it, "lights" the "candle," and begins to "mark" the "book" with the "pencil."

4. A patient gets into an "argument" with someone and shows him a passage in the "book" to prove his point.

5. Another patient gets into a "duel," using the "pencil" as a sword.

6. One patient put the chair on the table, got on the table, sat on the chair, put the "pencil" over his ear, lit the "candle," tore pages out of the "book," and set the "pages" on fire while singing bawdy songs.

This type of roleplaying must, of course, be seen to be appreciated. The enormous variety of responses possible is impressive and indicates well the range of human talent.

Another type of semi-structured situation which calls for interaction can also be used as a projective technique. The following instructions are given to Bob, who is to be tested.

> "Recently in the company where you work, your foreman (manager, supervisor, department head) has resigned. You think you should get the job. Your work record is good, you are taking night courses and instead of socializing with others you study a lot. Recently something has happened which makes the extra money very important. You need your job badly and you don't want to jeopardize it. You will meet Mr. M. and you will try to get him to promise you the job. See how well you can do."

Bob goes out of the room to plan his strategy and Mr. M. now enters. (He was out of the room while Bob was getting his instructions.)

> "Mr. M., we are going to do a bit of roleplaying. Bob works under your supervision. He is a good worker but he does not get along with the other men. They think he is rather pushy, overambitious, looks down on them, and in general, he disrupts morale. He just is not a good person in dealing with others.

Recently you learned that another firm is looking for someone at about the same salary and you know Bob could get the job, and that he would be better situated there. Your task is to see whether you can tactfully get Bob to quit and try for the other job. Keep in mind that he does good work but no one likes him. You really don't want to fire him, but you would be happy if he would quit."

This situation "tests" both participants. If the person playing Mr. M.'s role has played it a number of times, he tends to become a constant factor against which Bob can be measured. This dramatic situation can produce a wealth of information about a patient. Directors of roleplaying should develop one or more stock situations which will serve them as projective techniques. Over a period of time, as they see various people responding to the semi-structured situations, they will build up personal norms, which will help them evaluate new individuals.

It is well known that diagnoses are highly unreliable. Various studies indicate that even when very few diagnostic categories are employed, different observers will vary widely in the labels they assign to people.[1] Nevertheless, in many cases, therapy is probably accelerated if the therapist can get some idea of the nature of the problem faced by the patient, and some idea of the patient's idiosyncratic reaction to people and events. The question is which of the various diagnostic procedures is most useful in directing roleplaying-centered therapy. Both on theoretical and experimental grounds it would seem that roleplaying itself is the best kind of diagnostic procedure. Let us examine some of the more usual forms of diagnostic procedures.

The interview. Despite the almost universal employment of interviews for such purposes as deciding whom to hire, whether or not to accept a student, whether or not a person

[1] Ash, P. The reliability of psychiatric diagnoses. *Journal of Abnormal and Social Psychology,* 1949, 44, 272-276.

should be institutionalized, and so forth, the objective evidence is that interviews are both relatively unreliable and invalid. The reasons for this are evident. Most people are highly skilled at creating favorable impressions in short-range relationships. They know how to act in an interview. They have had considerable practice and preparation for creating good impressions. In the Kelly and Fiske research [2] of criteria for judging clinical trainees, the interview, even by skilled psychologists, was very disappointing as a means of assessing people.

Questionnaires. Personality questionnaires, such as the *Bernreuter* or the *Minnesota Multiphasic Personality Inventory* depend for their validity on a number of factors, including the honesty of the subjects, many of whom are not disposed to tell the truth about themselves. To accept the responses of individuals as truthful would be naive indeed. Even if the particular test has some means of determining the truthfulness of the individual's intentions, there is no way of knowing, if the evidence is that he did not try to lie, whether he was successful in "fudging" the test. If the evidence is that he did lie, then, of course, the results are not meaningful. In short, when one administers a test of the questionnaire type for any individual, results are rarely meaningful. Even more important, the diagnostician has no way of knowing how meaningful the results are for any specific individual. Besides, all such questionnaires can do is indicate what a person thinks about himself.

Projective tests. Procedures such as the *Thematic Apperception Test* or the *Rorschach Inkblot Technique* are only as valid and as reliable as the examiner. As is true of the interview, their value depends on who uses and who reports them. While for a time there was great hope that projective tests would act as X-rays into the psyche of people and bring forth hidden motivations, results have been highly disappointing.

Roleplaying. Whether roleplaying is better than other pro-

[2] Kelly, E. L., and Fiske, D. W. *The Prediction of Performance in Clinical Psychology.* Ann Arbor: University of Michigan Press, 1951.

cedures for understanding people is a moot point. The one solid bit of evidence in its favor comes from a research report by Borgatta [3] who found that roleplaying observations correlated more closely to real-life behavior than did paper-pencil projective techniques. That roleplaying observations should correspond more closely to real-life behavior than would the interview, or objective tests, or projective tests should be no surprise, since in general, on both theoretical and research bases, the more similar a test is to the function itself, the better is the degree of validity of measurement. Thus, we test a person's typewriting ability on a typewriter; how well a person swims by his performance in a swimming pool; and how well he handles social situations by observing him in the drawing room. Therefore, if we want to know how a person acts in relation to others, as when they tease him, we quite likely can find out best by a roleplaying test rather than by interviewing him, by asking him to fill out a questionnaire, or by asking him what he sees inkblots to be.

Why this is so should be evident. Roleplaying is a miniature representation of real life behavior. The person being evaluated faces stimuli to which he must respond in a spontaneous manner; he operates creatively, dealing with unexpected situations in a rapid manner. Usually, in a very short time, the enactment begins to have subjective validity and the subject becomes involved. He begins to operate in a totally committed manner and because he talks and moves, listens, thinks, feels, and reacts—all at the same time—he tends to become "himself" in the roleplaying scene. Quotes are put around "himself" because one has as many personalities as there are specific situations. Thus, while a patient is "himself" when he calmly tells how he behaved in a particular time and place—and gives a wrong impression—he is also "himself" if he is roleplaying this situation and gives a truthful representa-

[3] Borgatta, E. F. Analysis of Social Interaction: Actual, Roleplaying and Projective. *Journal of Abnormal and Social Psychology,* 1955, 51, 394-405.

tion of his real-life behavior. If the diagnostician wants to know *what* the person did in a certain behavior unit, he may find out via the interview; if he wishes to know *how* the person behaved, roleplaying will yield this information in a much more accurate manner as well as demonstrating *what* the patient did.

The patient referred to earlier told the truth as she saw it when she said that after her husband told her she could not have use of the family car, she did not argue, but merely went out of the room. But what we saw when she reenacted the drama was completely different from the impression she gave in the interview. That the interview impression was not a deliberate attempt at dissembling was evident since after she finished the roleplaying scene, she admitted that this is how the real scene had gone, and she had no idea that she could have given her husband a clear impression of irritation and anger.

An example of the relative validity of the interview and roleplaying against the criterion of real life behavior may be recounted.

An employer once sent a young sales trainee to the writer for evaluation. The employer stated that he was most highly impressed with the young man but that his functioning had been most disappointing. During the interview with the writer, the employee seemed quite at ease and he made a superior impression. He certainly seemed to have all the apparent personality qualifications for a salesman. However, to obtain a clearer view of the entire situation, the writer suggested that a complete sales situation be roleplayed. The employee, when the procedure was explained, namely, that he would open the door of an office, talk to the receptionist, get past the receptionist's desk, and then proceed to the interview, began to balk and his prior cooperativeness began to disappear. However, the writer persisted and the young man was asked to go out of the office, come in and talk to the writer, who now was to act the role of a receptionist. When this sales trainee entered, the writer, acting the role of the receptionist, began to ask who he was, etc. The trainee showed the greatest degree of distress. He was actually unable to talk! So extreme was the trainee's reaction that the writer believed that he had suddenly taken ill. However, when the trainee sat down he suddenly blurted out that he was completely unable to face receptionists! He confessed that he had many times gone into offices and if he didn't like the looks of the receptionist he just turned around and walked away. He had no trouble making a good sales presentation to prospects. He could deal with company presidents easily. But a seventeen-year-old girl receptionist who seemed unfriendly would cause him great distress.

The unexpected information, obtained by roleplaying, then led to some training sessions, during which the writer, acting as a receptionist, was eventually able to desensitize the sales trainee to receptionists. As a result he learned to meet receptionists, to get past them, and as a consequence, his sales performance improved. In precisely the same manner, the therapist who puts a patient into familiar situations can find out how the person acts and reacts not by a secondary method such as the interview, or a tertiary method such as projective techniques, but rather by a direct and close representation of reality.

« SUMMARY »

Roleplaying can be used to obtain information about how a person operates (his social personality) and how a person sees himself (his self-perception). Used with other diagnostic procedures, such as analysis of history, objective, and projective tests, the interview, etc., a more complete and presumably a more valid impression of the individual is obtained.

Information obtained by roleplaying is probably more accurate than that obtained by other means since it is more representative of real life behavior. This is because roleplaying tends to be veridical: the necessity for immediate responses to complex social stimuli tends to elicit usual rather than prepared behavior. The fact that the individual must think, feel, and act simultaneously tends to lead him to act in his usual rather than in some dissimulative manner.

When roleplaying is used for diagnostic purposes, the therapist is able to locate specific areas of difficulty, which in turn permits him to direct his attention to delimited areas of treatment. For roleplaying treatment, roleplaying diagnosis is most satisfactory.

« CHAPTER SIX »

Roleplaying for Instruction

THERE ARE TWO general ways of learning: passively, by attending to stimuli, as occurs in the classroom when one looks and listens; actively, by behavior, as occurs in the classroom when one actually does something. Thus, the child who watches the teacher write a letter on the board is learning in a passive mode; when he begins to use the pencil to imitate the teacher's production, he is learning in the active mode.

In psychotherapy, the patient also learns in the active and the passive modes. While listening to the therapist, while carefully attending to his explanations and interpretations, the patient is learning passively. While expressing himself or testing reality in the therapeutic situation, he is actively learning. In roleplaying, the same two processes occur. In general, when the patient is in the "audience" watching others, he is learning in the passive mode; when he is "on the stage," actually roleplaying himself, he is learning in the active mode. The situation is not necessarily simple, since a person can be active and passive at the same time. For example, he may be acting as an auxiliary ego and thus he is active, but his attention may be riveted on the hero, to see how the hero handles a particularly difficult situation, and in this sense he is learning in the passive mode.

One of the general points in group psychotherapy is that

everyone has a great deal in common, so that if an individual is talking about himself and his problems, what he is saying is likely to have considerable meaning to other individuals. This point has been called "spectator therapy" by J. L. Moreno. In roleplaying, when a member of a group acts out his problem, the situation is highly likely to be valuable and beneficial to the other members since they are likely to have similar problems. Just knowing that others share such problems can have some benefit; seeing how others handle their problems can be quite useful. Consequently, roleplaying done by others can be helpful to the observers due to the tendency of any person's problems to strike responsive chords in others.

In this chapter our concern is with learning in the passive mode—that is, by looking and listening. In the next chapter, the concentration will be on learning by doing. Let us now take a simple situation that might occur in individual therapy.

A patient complains that other people do not like him, treat him unfairly, etc. The therapist asks for a typical case, and let us say that the patient tells about an encounter with a roommate. Now the therapist asks: "Can we replay that situation?" And so the therapist and the patient roleplay the prior encounter. In this manner the therapist is getting diagnostic information about how the patient operates. Let us say that after the patient gets going in the situation his voice gets shrill, his language becomes immoderate, he interrupts, gets argumentative, etc. As a result, the therapist can "understand" the patient; that is to say, he begins to see the patient as the roommate sees him. His problem now is to help the patient "understand" himself. How can he do this? The most usual way is to tell a person. One could say, "You got pretty angry and you were very unpleasant. You raised your voice, you got over-emotional, and you became unreasonable . . ." But the message is not likely to sink in. One needs a more powerful stimulus to get the message across and roleplaying can provide this. The therapist may say: "Let us play the same situation over again. This time I'll play your role just as I saw you play it."

And so, the scene is repeated with the therapist now playing the role of the patient, just as the therapist saw the patient play it. The patient is now active, in that he is playing the role of his roommate, but he is learning in the passive mode because he is watching and listening to how he operates. In this manner the therapist can *show* the patient, rather than tell the patient how he operates.

The sociologist, Cooley,[1] posited the so-called "looking glass" concept of personality. He meant that we react to others who in turn reflect their impression of us by their behavior. But it is hard to understand what the "other"—the person who serves as a mirror to us—actually sees. The mirror technique in which an individual gets a chance to see himself as others see him tends to be both an intellectual and an emotional experience.

The tendency of people not to see themselves is illustrated by a humorous story. At a Christmas party some subordinates of a rather unusual supervisor decided to put on a skit in which one of them would portray him. They practiced and the person who was going to imitate the boss was a genius in mimicry, imitating the boss's voice, gestures, pet phrases, and behavior perfectly. The rehearsal was a mercilessly clear and devastating performance. At the party, when all were well lubricated with Christmas cheer, the skit was put on with the supervisor looking on. Some of the spectators who had not been in on the original planning were shocked by the accuracy of the performance and thought that the boss would be furious at being so cruelly lampooned.

The imitated person, however, was convulsed with laughter throughout the performance and after the scene was

[1] Cooley, C. H. *Human Nature and the Social Order*. New York: Charles Scribner's Sons, 1912.

over stated, "My, did you imitate an old windbag of a supervisor I once had. That is him, absolutely him."

« GROUP INSTRUCTION »

When an individual acts out his own problem this is called psychodrama. If, however, a problem is acted out in a group and has meaning to all of the members, the procedure is known as sociodrama. An example will make this clear. Let us assume that a group of married people is assembled and that all members have difficulty in dealing with their mates. Let us further assume that the group therapist desires to teach each member of the group how to handle a particular problem. He may operate in the following rather complex manner.

1. He posits a rather common problem in marriages, such as a difference of opinion about relating to an in-law.
2. The group may discuss the problem and how it should be handled.
3. Now, a couple may roleplay the situation indicating how they would actually handle the problem.
4. Each of the couples may now successively act out their method of handling the problem.
5. Further discussion may now occur about the various techniques. Ratings may be made of how well the various couples dealt with the particular problem.
6. Further replays may be made attempting to get every member of every couple to reach a satisfactory level of functioning.
7. The therapist may have cross-couple interactions so that the husband of couple one may interact with the wife of couple two, etc.

8. The therapist may himself act the role of a husband to show how he might behave in the situation.

We have here a complex situation in which a number of people with a common type of problem demonstrate to others how they behave and watch how others behave. On the basis of their combined judgments there is a tendency for the members of such a group to come to a more satisfactory solution of the problem than occurred at first.

In general, such procedures are an attempt by the therapist to show the patient or patients *how* to handle common situations. If this is done in individual therapy, the therapist demonstrates what he thinks the optimal method of operating might be. In group therapy, various individuals may, either on the basis of volunteering or as in the illustration, in terms of all showing how they would operate, indicate their method of dealing with a particular situation. While such situations may sometimes come from specific problems, in other cases they are general problems.

« SUMMARY »

Psychotherapy is a learning process and one learns by the passive mode of looking and listening as well as by the active mode of actually doing. In roleplaying, while it is more usual to think of people learning through direct participation, one can also learn in the passive mode by watching others operate. In some cases, it is too threatening for an individual to act out his problems and the therapist can lead him to more active participation by first employing "spectator therapy"—that is, by having problems similar to his own enacted. The more meaningful to the individual the problem played out, the greater the degree of involvement and the greater the degree of learning. In roleplaying for instruction the members who are acting serve as living audio-visual devices.

« CHAPTER SEVEN »

Roleplaying for Training

THERAPEUTIC ROLEPLAYING has a much more important function than either diagnosis or instruction. We call this process *training,* for want of a better word.

The reader may recall the case history of Al in which the patient, while roleplaying himself against his "father" ran out of the room. He got this idea in the heat of action, something which, as he put it later, had "never crossed my mind to do." The idea was a creation, a spontaneous act, a new behavior. As he got the impulse to run, and as he ran, he did not know its meaning. He had not as yet formulated the significance of this act. He acted, if one may use the term, impulsively. After repetition and after switching, it came to him that this "crazy behavior," which was what the frustrated father later labeled it, was sound, since it seemed to be the change point which improved matters for everybody.

Another illustration may be given, taken from a case I published elsewhere (17*). Manuel, a Mexican laborer, sexually molested a girl child, the daughter of a neighbor, and had been sent to prison for this crime. A man of forty, married and with children of his own, a hard working man of good reputation, he committed the act of exposing himself and fondling the child in the open, right in the street. When the child's father asked Manuel why he had acted in this

* See the Annotated Bibliography.

manner, Manuel told the father he did it because he wanted to and would do it again whenever he felt like it! The father called the police and in a short time Manuel was in prison.

Eventually, Manuel came into group therapy and after a number of weeks in the group, he reenacted a scene in which he, his wife, and his two sons went to see his (Manuel's) father in order to get the father's permission for the family to go to the movies. In the scene as enacted, the father refused to give his permission, and despite the complaining of his wife and sons, Manuel accepted the father's judgment and turned on his complaining children telling them that they should respect their grandfather.

In a subsequent discussion Manuel stated that he loved his father, respected him, and thought him to be the greatest person on earth. It was Manuel who had found his father dead. Manuel's grief had been extreme. Doctors had to keep him under sedation, so great was his sorrow.

The same roleplaying scene, referring to the movie, was repeated several times and again Manuel was unable to stand up to his father. With reluctance he repeated the scene a fifth time and on this fifth repetition, without the slightest warning, Manuel sprang forward, grabbed his "father" by the neck, threw him to the ground shouting obscenities, and was, with difficulty pried apart from the poor assistant who played the role of his father.

Manuel was dragged away and let lie on the floor while he raged and cried, beating the floor with his hands. After he quieted down a bit, he breathed deeply and spasmodically for several minutes with his mouth wide open, tears running down his face. At this point, all that could be said was that his sudden attack indicated that his attitude toward his father was really not the one he said it was and that the scene had had a powerful emotional effect.

But what is important is the sequel. At the next session, Manuel was able to tie together, at least to his own satisfaction, the meaning of his behavior of extreme bereavement following his father's death and his peculiar sex crime. He explained that he realized he had always resented his father and wished him dead, and that when he found his father dead his first thought had been, "I'm glad." He had put on the act of extreme sorrow and impressed everyone, but he *knew* he was glad. This conflict, together with his strict moralistic upbringing, required that he expiate the crime of wanting his father dead, and so he committed a most senseless sex crime to go to prison for punishment for his desire to have his father dead.

The above represents Manuel's own explanation and is not a statement by a sophisticated psychologist. Regardless of whether or not Manuel's explanation was true, it satisfied him and he felt better as a result of the drama he had played and in addition, was able to see himself in a somewhat different light in terms of his whole posture to life. He realized how dependent he had been on others, and how unable he had been to stand up to others.

These two cases, that of Al and that of Manuel, had to do with father-son problems and resulted in both individuals making certain central realignments. In one case, Al understood what to do to keep his father in line. In the other case, Manuel understood why he had committed the crime. And in both cases these central intellectual-emotional changes were dependent on the psychodramas. This is to say that insight, a central phenomenon, was the result of spontaneous action. In addition, improvements in feelings, subjective comfort, were attained.

Roleplaying therefore is a process of making inner gains, in insight and empathy, generalizations and motivations, self-confidence and peace of soul, and all of the usual subjective states of "mind," through peripheral, i.e., actional processes. Just as verbal psychotherapies aim at superior behavior by means of ratiocination, that is from within to outside, so too, roleplaying aims at greater subjective comfort and superior understanding from the outside to the inside.

The final goals of all therapies are more-or-less identical: to attain a superior level of understanding, increased subjective comfort, and better behavior. Surely no one would account a method of therapy satisfactory, if, for example, a person now understood why he behaved in some manner, and no longer felt uncomfortable, but his social behavior did not change. There is a joke which illustrates this point. A patient went into therapy because he was a bed wetter and after years of therapy stated that he still continued to wet the bed, but now understood why and no longer felt guilty! Just changing the inside is not enough.

These goals of understanding, comfort, and behavior change can be attained in different ways. The argument for roleplaying is that for some people, and for some problems, it is a faster and more economical method of change. Why is this so? In chapter two we have already discussed simultaneity, veridicality, and spontaneity, but now we have to consider this complex of forces against resistance. The common enemy of all personality changes is resistance, the inertia of people to change.

Personality tends to remain constant. If we have not seen a person for twenty years, it is remarkable how little he has changed in his thinking and behavior during this time. He is still himself. Unless there has been successful psychotherapy or some other powerful factors intervening, the individual, as he goes through life, is likely to retain a consistent personality. The patient in psychotherapy, despite his conscious desire to change, often fights therapy, i.e., change. He clings stubbornly to his ideas and to his behavior patterns.

In general, therapists' strategies are to lead and to direct change and still remain the patient's "friend." This process tends to create in the patient an ambivalent attitude toward the therapist. On the one hand he generally admires and trusts the therapist, and tends to get in a dependent relationship to various degrees; but on the other hand he resents the manipulation that the therapist engages in.

We come now to a theoretical notion of central importance. Which is better, to cut off a dog's tail at the base or to cut it off an inch at a time? Which is better, to make a total attack on a problem, handling the cognitive, emotional and behavioral aspects simultaneously, to make a massive assault on the problem all at once, or to proceed by easy stages?

To answer this, we should consider the consequences of "brutal" assaults. If a person is precariously perched on the edge of reality, certainly a cautious approach is indicated. If, however, the person has a "healthy ego," a more immediate and totalistic approach can be taken. Some psychotherapists, convinced that a slow, partial type of approach is necessary, conceive of man as highly unstable, and likely to "fall apart" by direct, frank confrontations, and so approach him, therapeutically, gingerly and cautiously. Others, more convinced of man's essential toughness and adjustability, approach him directly and forcefully.

We have here an example of a self-fulfilling prophecy. The timid therapist finds evidence for his point of view. The bold therapist also finds evidence for his point of view since both have successes. While roleplaying can be used tenderly or toughly, in general, its nature is such that it tends to be a rapid, i.e., a forceful method, and consequently is most appropriate for use by therapists who have confidence in patients' abilities to withstand the stresses inherent in roleplaying.

Do patients not differ in terms of their grasp on reality? If roleplaying is so rapid and so strong a procedure is there not danger in its use? Would not a therapist using this powerful method be likely to harm the patient?

The answer to these questions seems to be the following. People do differ in the degree to which they can take confrontation and violent emotional assaults, but in general, most patients are capable of dealing with such stresses. If the therapist is experienced and well trained, he has some degree of judgment about when and how to use roleplaying, and will have skill in controlling it. But the most important reason for not being concerned is simply this: psychotherapy is an interactive process but it is also an autochthonous process. The individual ordinarily absorbs only as much as he can. It is hard to overload the patient.

Therefore, the self-confident therapist who also has confidence in his patient, does not hesitate to use a powerful technique when he knows that his patient has control over the situation, and that the effect of roleplaying is limited by the patient's ability to handle any situation of this kind.

« PEAK EXPERIENCES »

One's life experiences generally run smoothly, with few traumas and surprises. But in each person's life, peak experiences occur. If one suddenly learns that a loved one is dying; if one is accepted by the school he wishes to attend; if a friend betrays him; if he suddenly wins a prize; if he learns that his money has been lost by the disastrous decline of a stock; if someone he desires tells him that the feeling of love is reciprocated—all these can be peak experiences. At such times, one is plunged either into the depths of a personal hell, or is raised exulting to heaven. These moments of despair, shock, wonder, bewilderment, ecstasy, tend to shake a person to his foundation. Unbearable anxiety, ineffable adoration, bewildering knowledge, indescribable terror, etc., are supreme tests of the intactness of personality. But all of them, no matter how deep the sorrow, how powerful the fear, how great the joy, are eventually absorbed and integrated by the organism.

But to some extent each of these events changes the person. Few people "snap" under strong shocks.

Successful roleplaying tends to elicit peak experiences. The individual is almost beyond himself in a really good psychotherapeutic session. He operates at maximal efficiency. Rage, tears, violent feelings occur. The person may blurt out what he never expected to say. He may act in unexpected ways. He may attain insights he never expected. The therapeutic experience can be almost unbearable. It is hard not to write dramatically about a method which does tend to produce dramatic events and dramatic consequences.

Lest the reader be a bit alarmed by all this, let it once again be emphasized that the nature and the extent of such reactions are a joint function of the influence of the therapist and the limitations imposed by the readiness of the patient.

« ROLEPLAYING FOR TRAINING »

The case of Manuel represents a type of violent reaction that occurs only under optimal conditions. Such peak experiences can be encouraged or discouraged by the therapist. More often, as shall be illustrated below, a patient can be trained by a number of roleplaying sessions, each designed to move the individual in a particular direction by easy stages.

The main concept here is that the roleplaying experience is real. If a person conquers a troublesome situation by practicing it in the safety of a therapeutic session, he gains self-confidence, assurance, skills, etc., almost as well as if he had encountered these experiences in real life. The person who has rehearsed real problems in an artificial environment has gained real insights, real assurance, and real skills which he can transfer to true-life situations.

Alvin states that he has great difficulty in dealing with

people. The therapist decides to use roleplaying. He sets up a series of exchanges between the patient and therapeutic assistants, graduating the scenes from easy to difficult, thus giving the patient veridical experiences in social interaction. He learns that the patient finds it easy to talk with a friend, more difficult to talk with a stranger, most difficult to talk with authority figures. Also, the nature of the conversation affects his ability. If the discussion is about trivia, this is no problem. If the issue has to do with something he wants, this is a bit more difficult; but if it is a conflict situation, this has the greatest amount of stress for him. We have now 3 x 3, or nine possibilities, ranging from talking trivia with a friend to a conflict situation with an authority figure.

The therapist assumes that the patient, if he is gradually led through the nine situations, and if he moves to a more difficult interaction situation as soon as he successfully experiences any one of them, will have gained confidence as he goes along, because these are veridical experiences. He will react to these play-acting situations in a realistic manner.

Nine situations such as *friend-wants something; stranger-trivia; authority figure-conflict* are sketched out. The scenes are to be graded in apparent difficulty for the patient. He is now to interact with someone (the therapist, or the therapist's assistant, if in individual therapy; with other patients, if in group therapy). After each scene is played, discussion will follow. If it is agreed that the scene was well handled, the next scene is to be played. If not handled satisfactorily a similar scene is developed, or the same one is repeated. After each scene, full discussion can take place, since between the scenes the patient may have many things, suggested by the roleplaying, to talk about.

We shall present some parts of some of the scenes.

FRIEND-TRIVIA

B: How are you, Alvin?
A: Pretty good.
B: Did you do anything on your vacation?
A: Yeah, we went away.
B: Where?
A: To the country.
B: Did you have a good time?
A: Pretty good.

T: How do you think you handled yourself in this roleplaying?
A: Well, not too good. I just don't know what to say. Seems like I'm scared.
T: What did you think, Ben?
B: Well, I really wanted to know how Alvin had spent his vacation. Getting an answer was like pulling teeth.
T: Perhaps we should repeat the scene. Alvin, you think you could play it a bit differently, perhaps imitating someone you know who you think could handle this type of situation better?
A: I loused it up. But let me try again.

B: Well, how are you?
A: Pretty good, thanks. And how are you?
B: Fine. I had a good summer. How was your vacation?
A: Swell. We went to the country.
B: Have fun?
A: Lots of it. Nice place. Very restful.

T: What do you think of Alvin's performance this time, Ben?
B: A little better. He showed some interest in me. Still not too much enthusiasm.
A: Let me try it again. I didn't really do it the way I wanted to.

B: How are things, Alvin?

A: I'm O.K. Had a good vacation. What did you do this summer?

B: The family went to the beach. I did a lot of swimming.

A: Me, too. We went to the country and there was a little pond and I did a lot of swimming. Also, for the first time in my life I did some horseback riding. I started on an old grey mare. She ambled along at about two miles an hour, and I sure enjoyed it. Ever ride a horse?

B: Not really . . .

T: Well, what do you think?

A: Much better. I felt more comfortable. I think I've solved that one. Let's go on to another.

FRIEND-CONFLICT

T: Well, we are now on a third scene. This will be with a friend and it will be a conflict situation. Can you give us an example?

A: Sure. Let us say that Ben wants to borrow my car and I don't want to let him have it.

T: How do you usually handle such a problem?

A: Badly. (All laugh.) I usually tell lies; I have to use it, or I have it in for repairs, or my father does not want me to lend it, or something. But usually, I end up lending it. But I want to be firm and polite and I end up being weak and polite.

T: O.K. Got the idea, Ben?

B: Yup.

B: Say, Alvin, can I borrow your car tonight?

A: No.

B: Why not?

A: (Getting excited.) I said "No." Isn't that enough? Don't you know what I mean? It's my car and I just don't want you to have it, that's all.

B: What kind of a friend are you, anyway?

A: Darn it, I have a right to say "No." You asked me and I told you "No." For god's sake can't you shut up!

T: Well, how was it?

A: Pretty bad. I didn't realize I could get so mad. I suppose I wasn't really mad at Ben but I was afraid I'd let him have the car, and so I took refuge by getting angry. I was firm, but not polite. How did I seem to you, Ben?

B: I felt you were insecure. You were trembling. I was pretty upset by your emotionalism. You were nervous.

A: It wasn't right. I suppose I'm just too weak to say "No" in the proper way.

We have at this point sampled a number of specific situations. Each one might run from two to five minutes. Depending on time, the therapist might carry over this sequence for a number of weeks. The period between sessions usually contributes to improvement, since patients tend to rehearse at these times. Let us sample two later sessions.

STRANGER-PERSONAL

T: Well, we have now worked out five of our situations. This time you will meet a stranger and get involved in some personal discussion. Any example from your experience, Alvin?

A: I sure have. Especially on a bus. I have been trying to start conversations and when strangers start to tell me their problems, I don't know how to handle myself.

T: Well, let us try and see how it looks. Ben, are you ready?

B: Yup. I got an idea how I'll do it.

A: Nice day.

B: What's so nice? It's raining.

A: Don't you like the rain?

B: You some kind of a nut? Who likes rain?

A: (After a period of silence. He seems hurt and baffled.) Well, the farmers do.

B: I ain't no farmer.

A: Neither am I.

B: So why do you say it's a nice day? (Turns his back to Alvin.)

A: (Breaking out of the role.) This is just what I am afraid of. People turning their back to me. What do I do now?

In the progression of scenes, each one becomes more and more difficult, and as Alvin succeeds in each one, he begins to gain confidence. As a consequence of the stresses placed on him, he begins to understand himself better, expanding his views of himself and others. Let us assume that Alvin has finally been able to solve this type of problem, which may take one, or many sessions, and let us hear what he might say during the non-roleplaying part of a therapeutic session.

A: Well, these scenes we have been playing have had a lot of effect on me. I feel so much better over all. My friends seem to like me more. I find it easy to talk to strangers. I'm even approaching people I never have talked to before. A couple of days ago, I went on a kind of a rampage. I just talked to everybody. I found out that most people, if you take the initiative, respond well. Most of them are like I used to be, that is they are scared of others. Just give them a chance and they'll talk to you.

T: You seem to have gained self-confidence.

A: I see I can talk to you, too. Why shouldn't I?

T: I'm not scaring you?

A: Well, no. I used to be scared of you. I'm as good as anybody, aren't I?

B: That's a broad statement.

A: Here's how I figure. I'm me! That's all there is to it. I have to live with myself.

T: Want to go ahead? We should move on to situation seven, trivia, with an authority figure.

A: No. We don't have to. I've been talking with teachers more and that's no problem. I've been having some conversations with policemen, too. What do you think of that? Yesterday I walked into a bank and I asked for the president. What do you think? They let me in to see him. I told him I was thinking of opening an account with them and I wanted to know if the bank was safe. He dealt with me very politely, and I didn't even feel scared.

T: Well, you *are* getting bold.

A: You know what? I am thinking maybe I ought to become a salesman. What do you think of that?

T: If that is what you want . . . Should we go on with the role-playing, or have you had enough?

A: I'd like to see how I do in a really tough one. Let's say I'm working and the boss calls me on the carpet. This actually happened. I worked once in a supermarket and the boss accused me of resting on the job. You would have thought I was guilty or something the way I just apologized. I know now how I'd handle that problem.

T: All right, tell me more about it so we can set it up.

B: I want to talk to you, Alvin.

A: Yes, Mr. Black.

B: I've been watching you work. You just don't seem to take any interest in your work.

A: Well, frankly, I don't really care for it too much. It's only a part-time job, but I put in time and effort. You have to admit that.

B: I don't know. It seems to me you haven't really been showing too much interest.

A: Like I told you, I don't see this as a career. Not that I think the job is beneath me, it just does not challenge me. Did you ever have to fill shelves?

B: Do you think I started at the top? I still fill shelves. A manager has to do everything.

A: Are you telling me I'm fired or are you warning me, or what? I'm willing to change if I can.

B: Well, that's the spirit. No, you aren't being fired. You are an aggressive guy, aren't you? I'd like you to put a little more snap to your work.

A: Maybe you're right. O.K., Mr. Black, I'll give my all for Super Deluxe Food Mart. I have a case of condensed milk that wants to go on the shelves.

B: Go to it, boy.

This extended example is given to show how roleplaying can be used as training in what seems to be a relatively innocuous situation. Alvin's former incapacity to communicate was only a symptom of a complex of attitudes and ideas. Symptom improvement means that underlying functions are improved, too. In roleplaying therapy, one finds that patients reap unexpected harvests; as for example, in this concluding discussion by Alvin after this series of dramas.

A: A lot has happened to me and I don't quite understand it all. I haven't talked much about my father, but we never really understood each other. Recently my relations improved with him. I am also doing better at school and I have made friends. I feel much better over all.

« SUMMARY »

The most important reason for using roleplaying as a psychotherapeutic technique is to initiate favorable "central changes"; i.e., thinking and feeling changes so that improved behavior will result. While there are many ways to attain this desired end, one relatively rapid way, highly effective in some cases, is to have the individual play himself in some interaction situation of sensitivity. The therapist and the assistants can manipulate the situation to create a peak type of experience in which considerable emotionalism will be displayed. This "breaking of the log jam" invariably is followed by insights and usually by feelings of comfort and by behavioral changes.

It is also possible to use roleplaying as a training technique, building up slowly, going from one stage to another, having the individual find success with some problem as he goes along, interspersing every situation with clarifying discussions.

While such scenes are in progress, the therapist continually gets diagnostic information, helpful to him in designing new situations, and if others who have problems are present, they get therapy in a vicarious manner from the information provided.

« CHAPTER EIGHT »

Roleplaying Centered Group Therapy

THE POINT HAS already been made that most psychotherapists, once they understand the procedures and values of roleplaying, will probably use it once in a while when it seems appropriate. Just as a carpenter or dentist has a variety of tools, each suitable for special purposes, so too the well-equipped therapist should have in his armamentarium a variety of procedures he can employ when needed.

However, some people may want to use roleplaying as their primary technique. It is possible for a therapist to do this in individual or in group psychotherapy.

Roleplaying centered group therapy or psychodramatic group therapy would be an example. While another exposition written in dramatic form is available,[1] to make our presentation complete, an example of a treatment method using roleplaying as the primary technique should be given.

« FORMAT OF ROLEPLAYING CENTERED GROUP THERAPY »

There are three independent ways of viewing this method.

1. From the chronological point of view—eight week cycles.

[1] Corsini, R. J. *Methods of Group Psychotherapy*. Chicago: William James Press, 1964, Chapter 15.

2. From the point of view of a patient—three-week cycles of intensive treatment.

3. In terms of a single session—of which there are two kinds.

CHRONOLOGY

Psychodramatic group therapy consists of an indefinite number of eight-week cycles. Seven successive sessions are devoted to roleplaying; the eighth session is leaderless and unstructured. In the first seven sessions, the leader is active, making all major decisions, except for two important areas: *who* is to roleplay and *what* he is to roleplay. On the eighth session, the leader submerges himself in the group, refuses to make decisions or assume authority, participating as an equal among equals.

The use of one non-directive session in the eight-week cycle is empirical. It provides relief from the considerable stresses of a highly structured and emotionally exhausting procedure of roleplaying; it provides a restful period in which people can demonstrate various facets of their personality, etc. Later in this chapter we shall discuss how both types of sessions operate and what tends to go on in them.

PATIENT CYCLE

During each of the seven sessions of the eight-week cycle in which roleplaying takes place, two patients are asked to volunteer to roleplay their problems on the following session. Since the typical group has from ten to fifteen members, twelve being probably optimal, each patient gets about one chance to appear during every eight-week cycle. When a new cycle rolls around, each member knows that sometime during the cycle, he should volunteer.

Let us say one cycle has ended and that this is the "relaxing, leaderless" session. Next week (if the group meets once weekly) two people are scheduled to roleplay. They had volunteered on the seventh session of the cycle. During the next session, the first of the new cycle, the other members are to consider whether they should volunteer for the following week. This deciding period is one of tension. No one likes to volunteer, and yet if no one does, the sessions cannot go on.

The period between volunteering and the actual roleplaying is of the greatest value to therapy. The typical patient gets into conflict of the approach-avoidance type. He wants to bring out something important to him and yet he is reluctant. He is in the process of examination of conscience, and this period of search and rejection tends to be one of tension, as the patient begins to formulate what he is to say and what he is to roleplay. Frequently, he decides to roleplay a rather innocuous situation, and then finds himself, during the actual session, discussing a more central and important problem.

Finally, the session in which he is to perform arrives. This is the second of the three-week cycle. He now tells his story and then he roleplays his problem. Immediately, on finishing the roleplaying, the patient is dismissed! He leaves the group and the group goes on to other things.

The period of one week between the moment he completes his roleplaying, and the next session in which he summarizes what the roleplaying means to him, is the most stressful period of all. Concluding the roleplaying, usually at a highly dramatic moment (as determined by the leader), he is suddenly expelled from the group, usually in a state of excitement and even of upset; he is now alone and faces himself. It is during this period of separation from the group that insight, comprehension, understanding, resolve, and rapid change tend to occur.

On the third session of the patient cycle, the patient listens to the impressions and opinions of the other members, each of whom, in round-robin fashion, makes a comment, and then he reports to the group his perception of the prior session and the effects of it. Following this, general discussion occurs.

This ends the patient cycle. After the leaderless session, if the patient remains in the group, he once again volunteers and once again goes through this three-week patient cycle.

Heightening of tension and anxiety is probably an important therapeutic facilitator. The patient before and after volunteering is engaged typically in a lot of soul searching. He feels anxious and uncomfortable because he knows other members will be attending closely to what he says and does. He desires to get help and to win the respect of others. He knows he will be the star performer only once in eight weeks, and he does not want to waste the session. On the other hand, he does not want to hurt himself too deeply and wants to avoid too intimate disclosures. Therapy is going on even before the roleplaying occurs. Roleplaying is the dramatic moment of truth, but it is not all of the therapy nor even most of it by any means.

The session in which he roleplays is typically short and usually traumatic. When the therapist ends the roleplaying, usually at the most dramatic moment, the patient is sent out of the group, excited and upset, still reverberating from the peak experience and usually he is in an uncomfortable situation. He has no one to talk to. Typically, he later reports that he was upset, felt his heart beating strongly, found he had no appetite, his sleep was affected, and the weight of all his past errors in thinking and behavior seemed to weigh on him. Eventually, before the start of the next session, he comes to some kind of peace, based on understanding or on decision, and so when he appears for the third session, he has prepared, as he knows he should, some kind of summary for the group.

Let us shift for a moment to the other members in relation to this three-week cycle of the patient. They watch him volunteer; they know from their own experience what he is going through during the pre-roleplaying week; and they know that they are going to be called upon to evaluate the patient. They have been with him for many weeks, they have experienced the roleplaying; some of them were therapeutic assistants in this patient's roleplaying. They, too, have some continuing anxiety in relation to what they are going to say. Each of them probably wants to help the patient and wants to show his insight into the problem and so this intervening week is one in which all of them tend to do some thinking about someone else.

The final session in which the patient summarizes and hears opinions can be as important as the roleplaying session. He may present some formulation about himself and his problem and then find no one agrees with him. A wild assortment of opinions, none of which may seem to have any validity, may be presented by the therapist and the patients. The patient is enveloped in a maze of contradictory opinions, some of which he may use in his next session as the basis of his new roleplaying.

While any one patient typically roleplays only once during the eight-week cycle, the entire period is active for the patient, not only in terms of his thinking about himself, but also in terms of his thinking about the dozen or so others. Everything is grist for the therapeutic mill.

THE ROLEPLAYING SESSION

The writer has found it valuable to begin each session promptly, and to end it just as promptly; to begin exactly on the minute and to end, if necessary, in the middle of a sentence, when the time is up.

The group is usually in a tight circle, or if a low stage is provided, in a semi-circle. The therapist conducts the roleplaying sessions in a business-like, no-nonsense manner. There is so much to be done, so little time! This attitude is soon felt by the patients and they too, soon get into the swing of things and operate with celerity. This mood of speed and impatience will be counteracted by the eighth leaderless session when relaxation is the rule.

On the therapist's agenda are seven points, some of which

may be skipped or may take only a few seconds to dispose of; others may take an hour or so.

1. Group business. This includes the introduction of any new member. Usually, only the new patient's name is given to the group; the names of the other members need not be revealed. The new member has always been interviewed at least once by the therapist, and if he is not a "one-session member" (professional person) he has been given a briefing by the therapist. He also agrees to attend at least three consecutive sessions before withdrawing.

2. Theory. The therapist may spend several minutes discussing some theoretical item, especially relating to roleplaying: what he is trying to do, how roleplayers should behave, the function of the therapist's assistant; perhaps a case history, etc. He should not, however, encourage questions, or spend too long a time on theoretical issues. Five minutes each session is about right for the theory section.

3. Patient summaries. The therapist says, "Mr. Smith roleplayed last week. Let us now go around and get opinions from each person." The patient at the therapist's right begins without any prompting and when he finishes his opinions, the next patient comments about Mr. Smith, who was the hero of the last session. And so on, without interruption. The therapist gives the concluding opinion. The person being analyzed frequently makes notes. The patient discussed now makes his comments and perhaps, rebuttals to what has been said, and then a general discussion occurs, stopped by the therapist after about ten minutes. The same recapitulation process goes on for the second patient of the week before and again the discussion is ended by the therapist. About thirty minutes have been used up by this time.

4. Roleplaying. The week before, two members volunteered. One of them now is asked to discuss his problem. The

drama to be acted is developed by the member, the therapist, and the group. Roleplaying assistants volunteer or are selected and they are briefed by the hero of the forthcoming drama. The hero goes out of the room while the therapist further prepares the group (to be explained in greater detail later in this chapter), and then the hero enters the room, the drama proceeds, and when the therapist thinks it best, he claps his hands twice to end the action, waves the hero out of the room, and then asks the next hero to begin his story. And the same process is repeated. This portion of the session usually takes about thirty to fifty minutes, leaving about ten to thirty minutes for the rest of the session.

5. Volunteering. Now the therapist asks for volunteers for the next session. He may select three; two for the next session and a "spare" in case one of the two volunteers may not show up. This usually takes about one minute. If volunteers do not arise, the therapist waits without comment. In some cases, he may wait in dead silence for as long as five minutes. He may, and should say, after five minutes of silence, "If we don't get volunteers, we will have to disband." If someone should volunteer who has recently roleplayed, the therapist may discourage him, saying, "We must distribute our time as equitably as possible. Let us wait until someone else announces that he is ready to volunteer." This attitude seems necessary for the group to operate. Unless a member will participate, there is no use having this procedure. This firm attitude by the therapist facilitates volunteering by reluctant patients.

6. Initiation. If a new member is present, one can be relatively certain that the intensity and fury of the roleplaying session will upset him, that he may be regretting he has promised to come for three sessions, and that all he wants to do is to be quiet and be allowed to withdraw without any notice of his existence being taken. Should he have, as sometimes happens, volunteered to participate during step four, he will be politely told that he cannot volunteer until he becomes a

full member. Ordinarily, the typical new member during his first session, feels inadequate, out of the group, and usually baffled and anxious. Now, he is going to get a shock. The therapist turns to him and says, "Mr. Yew, this is your first session. All new members are initiated. We have a prepared roleplaying situation which all of us have gone through. The situation occurs in a bar. We have a bartender, a customer in the bar, and you. The bartender is played by the newest member, and that is—oh, yes,—Mr. C., and the customer will be played by our next-to-newest member, and that is Mr. D. Please set up the bar." (The members mentioned set up a "bar" and the "bartender" goes through the motions of cleaning glasses, while the "customer" sits before the "bar" and goes through the pantomime of drinking.)

Typically, the new member, who has not been given the opportunity of declining, is probably wishing he were somewhere else, and is probably wondering how he got involved in all this. Then he hears the urgent voice of the therapist who seems *so* sure he will go through with the scene.

"Now, Mr. Yew, here is *your* problem. You are to go to the bar and order a drink. The bartender will serve you. We want to see whether you are able to open a conversation with the customer at the bar. You feel rather lonely and unhappy, and you sure would like to talk to someone.

"Everybody ready? O.K., Mr. Yew, do your stuff!"

And, so the new member gets up (in almost one hundred percent of the cases) and sits at the "bar." The "bartender" comes over and says in a friendly manner, "Good afternoon. What'll you have?"

The initiate usually asks for a "beer," and the bartender proceeds to open a "bottle" and "pour" it into a "glass," "deliver" it to the initiate, and perhaps say, "You're new around here," or "Nice day we're having," or something of the kind. Then he turns to serve some invisible customers, or perhaps the other "customer" at the bar. The initiate typically, at this time, is in sufficient control of himself to turn to the "customer" and attempt to start a conversation.

What happens from here on is usually hilarious. The "customer" was the "bartender" the last time a new initiate came in. And, the time before that *he* was the initiate. This means this is the third time that he has been in this situation; first as the initiate, then as the "bartender," and now as the "customer." So he has seen how two others have played the role of customer. This is his chance to use his ingenuity and spontaneity.

Among the various attitudes taken are: the "customer" wants to fight; he may try to borrow money; he will simply turn his back and refuse to talk; he may call the initiate an obscene name, or make an indecent suggestion, or mistake him for someone who owes him money, etc. In any case, the initiation is played for laughs, and the entire group is usually in hysterics by the time the therapist, keeping an eye on the clock, stops the action.

"Thank you for a splendid performance, Mr. Yew. When the next new member comes into the group, you will be the bartender, and the following time you will be the customer. Mr. C, who was the 'bartender' today will be the 'customer' next session."

This initiation has several purposes. Aronson and Mills [2] found in their research on cognitive dissonance, that if one suffers through an initiation, one tends to value what one has suffered for. Also, once a new member has "broken the ice" by roleplaying himself, he "catches on" to the idea, and is not so frightened. Also, now he feels that he belongs. He is one of the group.

7. The final step is an evaluation of the session either by the new member who has been initiated or by any visiting pro-

[2] Aronson, E., and Mills, J. The Effect of Severity of Initiation on Liking for a Group. *Journal of Abnormal and Social Psychology,* 1959, 59, 177-181.

fessional member. If the time is short, the therapist informs the person that he has "two minutes and thirty seconds," to give his opinions.

When time is up, the therapist rises and leaves the room, thus ending the session.

« THE LEADERLESS SESSION »

After seven sessions of the type discussed, the group meets again for a non-directed session. This time the therapist mostly sits and listens. He may smile, shrug his shoulders, or otherwise be relatively passive, letting the members find their own topics. Or, he may, acting as a member of the group, suggest any of a variety of topics for discussion, or he may ask general or specific questions.

Among the items that may be brought up are: the conduct of the meetings; how the sessions may be modified; how each person feels he is getting along; the evaluation of each patient by every other patient; theoretical issues of a general nature referring to "causes" of behavior or the "rationale" of the method; complaints, arguments, etc.

To use an inelegant word, the therapist strives for a bull-session, without plan or order, in which people do not bring up personal problems necessarily but discuss themselves as a group, or discuss the progress of others. People who want to leave the group should announce it at this time. Discussion of the wisdom of any patient leaving the group usually takes place at this session. The therapist strives to keep his silence, and not dominate the group. He clarifies, asks questions, makes *short* general comments. He is one of the "bunch" and nothing else.

Above all, he must not be defensive. He answers any questions honestly. He criticizes himself. He explains patiently. He may criticize others. Since he is a member of the group and is not in a privileged position, he speaks out his mind and may even attack someone in the group. He may talk about himself in relation to how he functions in the group, etc.

Such sessions are helpful, and, of course, the purpose of these non-directed leaderless sessions should be explained (during step two, the theoretical part of the roleplaying session), so that everyone will understand what is to come and how to act.

The next session begins the first roleplaying meeting of the new cycle.

« A SESSION IN ACTION »

Below we shall give highlights of a typical but fictitious session. The leader is symbolized as T, and the members are A, B, C, ... M. The session begins at four p.m. and ends at five-thirty p.m.

4:00

T: O.K., it is time to begin. I'd like to introduce Mr. Lee, a new member. I have explained the nature of the group to him and he is on a probationary status for three weeks. I'd like to announce also that Mr. K has come again this week, and that since this is his fourth session, he can be considered a regular member.

4:02

Now let me talk a couple of minutes about the role of the therapist's assistant—the antagonist. The person who is the main actor is known as the hero. The assistant has a very tough job. He must generate, in the mind of the hero, the person he is portraying. Usually we do quite well. But do you know why last week F was able to say to B, "You really acted just like my mother!"? There are several reasons. First, do you realize that you are a constant stimulus to others? People don't just act; they react. So, when F thought that B acted just like his mother, it probably means that F acts in a particular manner and his mother and B react to him in the same way. The assistant has to be quick to understand both the hero and the person he portrays. Before roleplaying ask the hero questions, find out what words the hero's antagonist uses; in this way you can really get into the role you are playing. Be ready to modify your approach, don't hesitate to shift your position. Listen carefully to the hero. When he begins to get involved you can almost feel his emotionalism, and then you know you are striking pay dirt.

4:08

T: Well, let us get on with the analysis and summary of last week's session. Mr. D, you were the first subject last week, so let us go around.

K: I got the impression that D is still too dependent on his mother. He is scared of her.

A: Me, too. Secretly he admires her strength and wants to be like her. I don't think he really cares for his father.

B: Well, I don't know. I think he is scared of both. He doesn't want to be like his father, but he doesn't want to be like his mother, either. It seems to me he can't find himself and so is trying out different personalities. He changes so much. (Others also comment.)

4:11

T: Well, now we have heard from eleven people and it is up to you, Mr. D. What do you think of what was said?

D: I am absolutely amazed how wrong you all are. God, what absolute nonsense. Where do you come to such ideas? After I left the room last week I cried. I realized how much I hurt my mother. C was correct when he said I'd spent too much time hurting her. I guess I am angry with how she has been picking on my father and me. I realized, well, I realized I didn't like either of them. Maybe you are right. I don't know, the whole thing is confusing to me.

T: Well, all is up in the air. We'll come back to you in a couple of weeks or so, Mr. D. And now, let us go over Mr. J's case which was the other psychodrama last week.

4:26

T: And now we come to our first case for today, Mr. M. You have the floor, sir.

M: I was brought up by a dog. Really. We had a St. Bernard. I used to sleep with her; I'd go out with her. She was my baby sitter. The thing I want to go over may sound crazy, but that dog was like a mother to me, seemed more real than my real mother. She died at an advanced age. She was brought into the house when she was a puppy and I was about two. When she died . . . (goes on narrating).

T: Well, how can we dramatize the problem?

M: I'm not sure.

T: What do you think?

M: If someone could act Goldie's part . . .

T: O.K. A dog has a personality too. You loved Goldie. Who do you think could play her part?

(Roleplaying takes place.)

4:32

M(M): I've lost my mother. (Cries.) I have no one.

T: (Slaps hands.) That's it. Out you go, Mr. M. And let us go on to our new subject, Mr. F. Please begin.

4:47-5:06 (F's roleplaying takes place.)

5:07

T: O.K. We need volunteers for the next session. K is first. He volunteered last week. We need two more, one to follow K and one for standby. Let's not waste time. We have an initiation to do.

A: I'll volunteer.

T: Weren't you on recently?

A: Two weeks ago.

T: Maybe you ought to wait.

E: I'll volunteer.

T: Good. One more please.

H: I think I'll volunteer.

T: O.K. E for next week, with H standing by.

5:08

T: Mr. Lee, this was your first session, and I suppose all this seems kind of strange and upsetting. We run a kind of a skit. Mr. F is our last member. He is going to play the part of a bartender and our next-to-last member is . . .

H: Me. I play the "customer."

T: Fine. Now, see they are setting up this "bar." Mr. F is going to serve Mr. H a drink. You are going to the bar, and ask for a drink, too.

L: I don't drink.

T: You can ask for soda water, a lemonade, or whatever. But here is your problem. You feel lonely and you'd like to talk to someone. Now, you are to try to strike up a conversation with Mr. H, the "customer." See if you are able to get him to talk to you. O.K.? Go ahead.

L: (Walks to bar, uncertainly.) Do you carry cold soda?

F: Sure, lemon pop, or ginger ale, or root beer.

L: You have a coke?

F: Only in the quart size. The little ones are gone.

L: Well, let me have a ginger ale.

F: They are only in quarts. Want a beer?

L: No. What is in the small size?

F: How about a lemon?

L: Good. (F opens a "bottle," sets it before L, puts a "glass" on top of the "bar,' and turns to H.)

F: Want a refill, Harry?

H: Sure, same . . .

L: (Hestitantly.) Is your name Harry?

H: What's it to you?

L: Nothing.

H: So why did you ask?

L: I had a dog named Harry.

H: What are you, a wise guy?

L: No. I didn't mean anything. Just want to talk.

H: Don't bother me. I know your kind.

L: What do you mean, my kind?

H: You know what I mean, a moocher. Don't have money to buy a real drink. A moocher, that's what you are. Isn't he a moocher, Fred?

F: Now, Harry, this guy only asked you your name. No use getting sore. (To L.) Harry is kinda touchy sometimes when he drinks too much . . .

L: Sorry, Harry. I meant no offense.

H: (Gets up, takes off his jacket.) You want to fight? I hate moochers.

5:26

T: Well, we had a lot of fun, Mr. Lee, and I hope you enjoyed the skit. When we get our next new member, you will play the "bartender" and Fred will play the "customer" and the time after you'll get a chance to play the "customer." But, seriously, we would like to get your impression of our meeting. We end in three minutes.

L: I don't know. It is quite an experience. I didn't really know what it was all about. The two men who playacted, I wonder why they were sent out of the room. The second man—the one with the dog—that was a weird story. He was actually crying. I don't think I could ever tell such things about myself—trying to have sex with a dog . . . But, I am impressed how you all work together. I don't know if this group is for me. I thought psychotherapy would be different. I don't know if I can take it.

T: We'll see. After you have come three sessions you can make up your mind. I think most of the fellows and girls here felt the same way you do now at first. Well, there's fifteen seconds to go. Anyone want to say anything? No . . . ? It's now five-thirty. See you next week, same time. (Gets up to leave.)

« SUMMARY »

While a full explanation of psychodramatic group therapy is beyond the scope of this book, it is based on several fundamental conceptions. One is the use of alternation of vectors. There are eight sessions to each cycle—seven of a rapid, dynamic structured type, dominated by the therapist, and one relaxed and leaderless. The patient at one moment can be surrounded by others and a moment later he may be out of the room alone. Roleplaying scenes can range from the most serious problems to a burlesque initiation. The therapist is kind and soft at times, rigid and uncompromising at others.

All these "pushes" and "pulls" tend to have the effect of making this form of group therapy rather dynamic; generating a feeling of excitement and movement.

Another concept involves sending a person out of the group immediately after a crisis occurs. The patient is left strictly alone to work out the problem on his own. This rather "brutal" technique seems to have good effects in terms of new insights (18 *). The theoretical explanation is that by this procedure a kind of incomplete Gestalt occurs. The person is upset and wants to find answers to reduce his discomfort. He works out the problem best alone.

Still another element has to do with the week between the psychodrama and the recapitulation. The interim week permits the patient to do some hard, deep thinking. The knowledge that each person will be called on to give his opinion about the previous week's drama, motivates patients to try to understand the problem faced by the main actor of that session.

* See the Annotated Bibliography.

« CHAPTER NINE »

A Case Example of Psychodramatic Group Therapy

THIS IS AN example of roleplaying in a therapeutic group with a "peak experience" leading to dramatic results which the writer has labeled "immediate therapy."

The locale was a prison. Ben, the hero of this case study, had a curious prison history. Despite the fact that he had once escaped and had been recaptured, he so favorably impressed prison officials that he had been assigned one of the most responsible jobs in the institution—managing a prison store which sold inmate-made trinkets and novelties to the public. In this job he handled a considerable amount of cash.

Ben was thirty-eight, a quiet, self-contained person who impressed one by his modest, sincere manner. A house painter by trade, his criminal history included a number of alcoholic binges during which he would throw away all his money buying drinks for strangers. When his money was gone he would write checks, signing his own name and continuing even when his checking account was empty. He had been arrested, convicted of forgery, put on probation, repeated this senseless behavior, sent to prison; released after a year on parole, repeated the behavior, and again returned to prison. When released he had always worked and even though not under legal obligation to do so, "having paid his debt to society," he would locate stores that he had defrauded and pay his bad checks.

In short, he was a neurotic criminal, and there was no

evidence of any real attempt on his part to defraud. This persistent self-defeating neurotic type of behavior had been going on for more than ten years and he had been jailed and imprisoned several times when he finally wended his way to psychodramatic group therapy, the complex version of therapeutic roleplaying described in the prior chapter.

Ben told the following story to the group after attending sessions for several weeks.

B: Every once in a while I go out on a drunk, and I begin throwing my money away. I buy drinks for everybody. This may go one two or three days. I've given away up to a thousand dollars in a weekend. When I am broke, I go back to the saloons I've been in and again I buy drinks for everybody. When the bartender asks me to pay, I give him a check and then go on to the next bar. The bartender welcomes me, for after all, maybe yesterday I gave him one or two hundred dollars in cash—and I'm a good time Charlie and sure enough he takes a check when I tell him I am broke. Now, maybe after this binge I go back to work, go back to the bartenders, and begin to pay them off. But maybe they begin to call in the cops, and I am soon back in jail. I just have no idea why I behave in this manner. That's why I'm here.

T: How about your early life?

B: I never think of it.

T: Did you have parents?

B: My mother died when my sister—she is a year younger than me—was born. My father brought us up.

T: What was your father like?

B: A religious fanatic. No one could bring drink into the house. He was always reading the Bible. We had to memorize it. We couldn't have a radio. No fun in the house. Just prayer meetings, reading the Bible. I couldn't play with other kids; just work and religion.

T: What happened to your sister?

B: She—she is in an insane asylum; been there a long time. I just heard about it; never visited her, never wrote to her.

T: Ever married?

B: Me! No! I stick to myself. No friends.

T: Did your father have friends?

B: None. He wouldn't let anyone in the house.

T: Did he smoke?

B: That was worse than drinking. You went straight to hell if you smoked. Only those who had the devil in them brought fire into their lungs.

T: Do you smoke?

B: Never did.

T: Do you remember anything about your early life?

B: I don't like to think about it.

T: Tell us about an incident you remember.

B: What's the use? I told you it was just unhappy. I don't have a single happy memory. Don't want to think about it.

T: I understand, but you must understand that you'll help yourself if you'll tell us more about your early life. Does any one memory come to you?

B: I don't know why you want to know. There's no good in it.

T: A situation which involves you, your sister, and your father . . .

B: I remember once he beat me.

T: Describe your father. How did he look; how did he act; how did he think?

B: He was a tall man. Very straight and tall. Never smiled. Serious. Low voice except when he got angry. Would go into fits—rages. Threw chairs about. Scared me. Threatened me with everlasting hell fire. I was scared of him.

T: And your sister . . .

B: A sneak. She tried to make me out to be bad. "You'll go to hell," she'd tell me. "You don't read the good book." This day I remember I came home from school late. School was out at three and I knew my father wouldn't get home until six. So I watched some kids playing ball. Must have watched an hour. When I got home my sister said, "I'm going to tell father." I begged her not to. I promised her things. She said she'd tell him. I tried to get her to lie. Father hated liars; they would go straight to hell . . .

T: And then . . .

B: I read the Bible and my father came in and I was scared and Cathy, she told him and he asked me and I told him I watched the game and I wanted to be like others. And he beat me. (Seems upset.)

T: O.K. Let's get you a sister. Who do you think can imitate her?

B: I don't know. Anybody, I guess.

T: Who wants to volunteer?

C: I had a sister just like that. I'll do it.

T: And the father?

D: I'll take the part. (This volunteer was a visitor to the group; a young psychiatrist in residency training. This was his first experience in therapeutic roleplaying.)

T: All right, Ben. This is your "sister." Tell her more about herself so that "she" will know how to play "her" role.

B: She . . .

T: No. Say "you.' Make out that C is your sister.

B: You are a year younger than me. Your name is Cathy. You are about nine years old and I'm ten. You always try to make me bad!

C: How do I talk?

B: Like this. "Ben, you're bad. You're going to hell. I'm going to tell father on you. He'll fix you, so you'll see."

T: And now tell "Father,"—Dr. D, what your father was like.

B: You look something like my father—stern, angry, mean. You talk in a soft voice, but it scares me. You look like you might kill me. I'm scared of you.

T: All right. Here's how it'll go. Ben, you will leave the room. When you come in you'll see your "sister." You know you have done wrong coming home late and you know she'll tell your father. You are scared. You and she will have a talk.

Then your father will come in, and you and your father will have a talk. While waiting outside, try to get the same feeling you had as a kid. (Ben goes out.)

T: Now, let us make this a good one. C, you have to probe to see what upsets him. Remember to say "I'll tell Father," "You'll go to hell," . . . O.K.?

C: I got it.

T: Dr. D., the point of this psychodrama of Ben's is to really get into the role. Righteous indignation, absolute belief in hell, love and concern for your son who is going into sinful ways; you'll have to play it by ear.

D: That's easy. My father was like that.

T: Audience, now please, be as quiet as possible. Watch and listen carefully. Next week we'll analyze. O.K., everybody, let's roll. Call Ben in.

B: (Enters. Somewhat uncertain.)

C: Where have you been? It's almost five o'clock. You should have been home long ago. You know Father wants you to come home right after school.

B: I was watching the boys play ball.

C: Oh, that is a sin. Wait till I tell Father. Watching a ball game.

B: Don't tell Father! (Voice raised.)

C: You're going to go to hell. Oh, won't father fix you. You'll see. You will see!

B: What's wrong with that? Always cooped up in this apartment. Only permitted to go to school. (Shouts.) And I never play like other kids.

C: You're shouting!

B: (Screams.) Yes! I'm shouting, I'm shouting. I'm different from all the kids. Why! Why! Why!

T: (Motions to D.)

D: (Enters, and Ben stops shouting. D speaks in a low deliberate voice.) What is going on?

C: He came home late, Father. Watching a ball game.

D: (In a whisper.) A ball game?

B: Yes.

D: A ball game! (Speaks louder.)

B: (Suddenly. Screaming again.) Yes. I did. Just stopped. Nothing wrong. I just watched. I didn't play.

D: (In a menacing whisper.) Get the good book. (Fixes his eyes on Ben. Ben follows in the line of D's finger and gets a book. D stretches out his hand for the book and Ben hands it to him. D kisses the book and hands it to Ben.) Swear to God almighty that you'll never, never again see a ball game. SWEAR! (Shouts, his face contorting.)

B: NO! (Throws book on the floor.) NO!

D: Bastard! (Suddenly whips off his belt and begins to beat Ben who falls on the floor, crawling under chairs, knocking chairs in all directions. Ben screams in terror while D is bellowing "BASTARD! DAMNED ONE" and continuing to beat Ben with his belt. Meanwhile the "sister" is screaming.)

T: (Slapping hands twice.) Stop! (C and D resume their places in the circle while Ben, groveling on the floor, chairs over him, is sobbing. The group is frozen into silence, the therapist puts a finger to his lips to caution continued silence. Eventually Ben arises, tears streaming down his face, and sees the therapist pointing to the door. Looking like a pathetic boy, he limps to the door and goes out of the room.)

T: O.K. Now, after this pleasant domestic scene, let us go on to our next problem. J, I think it was your turn.

J: Well, this is my problem . . .

ANALYSIS

Evidently, Ben was not a professional criminal. His self-defeating behavior was certainly related to his unusual childhood. His drinking habits and his wasting of money were probably symbolic acts of defiance of his implacable moralistic father. The fact that his only sister was in a mental hospital was further evidence of the father's effect on the children.

The intent of the therapist was to open up an old wound, to let the pus out, to relieve the toxic effects of the traumas of the past.

Ben knew well where the "wound" was, where the pain was greatest, and despite his early reluctance, he did give data on which a psychodrama could be built. When the action started, in a matter of less than a minute, the scene had become psychologically real—veridical for him. He talked in a frightened manner. His psychological reality was intensified by the empathic behavior of C (playing the sister he had had who was like Ben's sister) and by the acting of D (who had had a father like Ben's).

The short drama rose to a rapid boil, and when D unexpectedly took his belt and began to beat Ben, he was really angry, since the scene had become real for him too. And C acting the sister got so in the role that he screamed from sheer terror. The whole drama had an unbearable intensity for Ben who lost his control, falling down, crawling under chairs, and screaming with fright and pain from the blows of the belt.

SECOND SESSION

Let us now proceed to the next session. Ben is talking, having asked to speak first.

B: Well, I want to tell you all what the last week's session meant to me. Nothing like this ever happened to me. When I left the room, I just stayed in the hall for a time. I didn't want no one to see me. I was pretty upset, you know. I just sat in the hall. After a time I got up and went back. I was shaky all over, like I was sick. I got to my bed and lay down. I couldn't think. I couldn't control my mind. I kept seeing myself as a kid. My fear of my father. My sister I just saw there in my mind like pictures flashing by, you know. Somebody came by and asked me, "You going to eat?". But I just shook my head and I didn't eat for two days. No appetite. Didn't sleep. Dreams, all crazy like. Just went on like I was sick. Didn't answer anyone. Just dopey. Kept tightening my fists and wanting to hit someone. And, yet, crazy like it seemed, I felt good. A weight had gone. I tried to understand it. I realized I didn't hate my father any more. You see, I could see him in his coffin, with his hands folded on his chest, and his Bible in his hands, and I saw the flesh on his hands turning green, and the flesh falling off and he became a skeleton and I was glad he was dead, and suddenly I felt "He's dead" and I'm free and he's dead and I am not afraid of him. And then I felt free. And then I felt sorry; I knew he was an unhappy man. Maybe he loved our mother. Maybe he really believed in the book. Maybe he was doing what he thought was right. Am doing a lot of talking, thinking fast. Not used to this. Have to explain. Give me time, please.

T: All the time you want . . .

B: Like I felt sorry for him, more sorry than I ever felt. I loved my father. Good man, harsh and strict, but a good man. Loved us in his way. Wanted us to be god-fearing. I hated him. Wanted to spite him. Drank and didn't like it. Felt I was a sinner, spent my money. Get rid of it. Get punished. Get arrested. All this make sense to anybody? (Looks around, several heads nod understanding.) Well, then I calmed down and then got excited again, but I felt sorry for Cathy. Wrote to her. First time. Want to see her. She was victim too of my—crazy father. We're all crazy; me, my way; he, his way; she, her way. All of us crazy.

Now I see it. More relaxed. Understand. Father good, but sick. I'm good, but sick. Cathy was scared. My drinking, check writing, all due to my sickness. My god, I can't stop talking, I . . .

T: You can stop talking, especially since we are going to talk about you, Ben. Would you like to listen to what we think?

B: Sure. Yes, I can listen.

T: O.K. A, how do you feel about the whole thing?

A: Well, Ben sure got a jolt last session. Like a shot of morphine.

I never heard him talk so much. I don't know if it cured anything, but he sure has changed. That was quite a session. I think he has finally decided to stop drinking.

C: Well, I played the sister, you all know. I got really scared of Ben's intensity. And D, he really came across. When he pulled off the belt and started laying into Ben, well, screams just started coming out of my mouth. You know I've been in this group longer than anyone except Dr. T, of course, and I can say this: we really got to Ben. I don't know if all this will change him but I know he won't be the same after this.

D: Well, I have a confession to make. I mentioned my father was like B's, and I, like Ben, didn't really like my father, and I have become something like him. When Ben threw down the book I became my father—his father. I lost my head and I had not thought before of taking off my belt. Next thing I knew it was in my hands. By the way, did I hurt you?

B: I didn't feel a thing until the next day.

D: Sorry.

T: That's nothing, Doctor. You did what you felt was right.

D: Well, it was a peak experience for me and it was therapeutic. My father lives with me; he's a semi-invalid and since the psychodrama I've been much more kind to him. So the role-playing had an effect on me, too.

E: Last week was my first time. I didn't talk about this to anyone since I suppose everything that goes on here is confidential, but I know one thing. I want no part of this business for myself. It's all kind of crazy. Just keep me out of this, that's all I got to say.

F: My impression is that Ben has changed and for the better. He had something inside him, like a cancer that had to come out. He finally got it out of himself, hatred of his father. I don't understand why this procedure did it, but I think it did. Ben will never be the same again. I got an idea he'll be a changed man. It took a lot of guts for him to go through that experience.

G: I've been thinking about Ben all week long and I am sorry to say I don't agree with any of you. I think he's conning us and possibly fooling himself, too. All this talk about hating fathers. Well, I got some kids and I bring them up strict and my father beat me a lot too, and I don't hate him. I don't get all this talk.

H: I disagree with you, Mr. G. The experience was valuable to me and I was only an onlooker. My father died when I was small and I was brought up by my mother and she was something like Ben's father, and I felt for him. I think he's let the hatred out of his soul, and he now can examine himself, and that he can begin to build a good life. I don't think the therapy is over but it's a start.

T: Well, we've had all kinds of opinions about Ben and in a moment we'll let him respond. As I see it, Ben went through a crisis period in this room last week. Now he has made some personal sense out of it. How do you respond to what the others are saying?

B: I'm more calm now. Am glad to hear your opinions. I think I lost the hatred in my soul for my father. You see, I guess I believe in hell and all that and I went around hating him and hating myself for hating him and for hating my sister. I really don't hate, just feel sorry and I wrote yesterday to my sister and I hope she can read my letter and that she is alive. I'm going to take care of her. She has no place to go. We have no relatives. My father was an orphan, brought up in a religious orphanage, and maybe that's where he got how he was, poor guy. I believe I'm all through with the drinking. I was not an alcoholic; just was trying to kill myself, throwing away all my money.

T: O.K., we have to go on to the recapitulation of J's roleplaying. Can you tell us about the meaning of your session?

J: Well, last week, I . . .

« SUMMARY »

The reader may get the impression that a psychodramatic experience can be a "one shot" therapy. This seems to be not far from the truth. In cases such as those of Manuel and Ben that we have just reported, individuals seem to come up with relatively lasting insights, relaxed emotional states, and changed behavior after one session of this kind.

Since this concept of "immediate therapy" is relatively new, a few words may help to explain how and why such peak experiences occur in psychodramatic group therapy. One must remember the many pressures put on group members in psychodramatic group therapy. First, they see others acting out emotional situations. This tends to give them courage to also bring forth sensitive issues. Next, each patient knows he gets only one chance to act out a problem every eight weeks. This creates a "now or never" attitude. The discussions following each session in which every patient is raised to the status of a therapist tend to give each person an investment in the group process. The "push and pull" attitude of the therapist and the structure of the sessions with this crowded agenda and no-nonsense air tend also to facilitate matters. There are also other factors: the tension prior to volunteering; the week of waiting and the thinking about what to bring up; the release when one begins to tell one's story; the selection and volunteering of antagonists; the structuring of the situation; the getting into the mood while waiting, and then entering the room; getting involved with people who become the ones one has dealt with; the mechanisms of spontaneity as one talks and interacts; the simultaneous summating effect of intellect, emotions, and behavior; and the sense of reality so great that the antagonists look and act like the real people (creating a sense of veridicality). All these combined with the pain of the tension and the hope of peace, tend to create a sense of total involvement leading to an explosive climax in which all control is lost—the unbearable moment of final truth—and then, hands are slapped twice, the fantasy dissolves, and one leaves the room, alone.

This is how the typical patient reports his experience. Out of the group, all alone, filled with churning emotions, loss of identity, traumatic separation, physical upset, thoughts crowding, a storm in the brain, heart beating wildly, visions, memories crowding madly, unable to think, in a state of fatigue and yet alert, thoughts keep intruding, ideas keep forming, on and on, one's miserable life begins to shape up. One begins to get flashes of understanding. Sharp and recurring thoughts. One tries to escape, but there is no escape. Words in print are meaningless. One walks and talks and yet the mind is racing. That damned thought comes back, it comes back. No, it can't be. But it comes back. Yes, that's it. Let me be courageous and face it. This is the reason. Be honest, this is it. And then comes peace. One sleeps. One is calm. One has accepted the truth. One is now well.

The above dramatic language is an attempt to summarize, to give the essence of what subjects report after a really dramatic session.

« CHAPTER TEN »

A Case Example of Roleplaying in Individual Psychotherapy

BELOW WILL BE RECOUNTED a case history of a young woman treated in individual therapy by conventional means: directed interviews, permitting her to recount instances of her behavior and that of others, interpretations, and also by roleplaying, which seems to have been the means which hastened an apparently successful conclusion.

Mildred was a self-initiated patient, who called me for an interview the day after she had heard me give a lecture. We talked on the telephone for a while, but she would give me no information at that time about the nature of her problem, stating that she wanted to discuss the matter in my office.

FIRST INTERVIEW

My first impression was of a somewhat unattractive woman in her mid-thirties. She wore glasses and had protruding teeth. She was dressed in a somewhat unattractive style and had a patently no-nonsense and practical way about her.

In answer to my question: "Will you kindly tell me what is the reason for coming to see me?" she replied somewhat as follows.

M: For some time I have been thinking about coming to somebody for advice about myself, and I made up my mind to see you when I heard you talk. The truth is that I have many personal problems. I am simply unhappy and feel that life is passing me by. I am thirty-three, I am single, and I live in an apartment with three roommates. I have been living on my own, even though my parents live in this city, and in the past eight years since I graduated I have had any number of roommates get married and set up their own homes.

I work as a research biologist for a pharmaceutical company and have been with this company since I got a Master's degree eight years ago. I have a younger married sister who has two children. I earn a good salary, have gotten regular increments, and I think I'm well regarded by my supervisor, even though I don't think my work is very meaningful nor the quality of what I do is too good.

Right now what concerns me is that my roommates get dates; they have men calling them all the time. I have not gone out on a date for almost a year. During all of my five years in college I had only one date—at the senior prom.

I know I'm not too attractive and that I have too high standards. But something about me repels men, I suppose.

What I want, simply, is to get married. Unless I meet suitable men, I can't have dates and I can't marry. All eligible men at my age seem either to be married or to be peculiar in some way or other.

I suppose I have a psychological problem of some kind. That is why I am here.

We continued our conversation, and at the end of the hour it seemed that her problem was indeed, as she said, psychological; i.e., it had to do with her concepts of self and her behavior related to her feelings and ideas about herself, as well as to her habits, and I agreed to see her as a patient.

We spent several weeks in obtaining a detailed developmental history. I learned that over the past eight years she had had a total of about forty dates with about ten men, most of whom dated her once or twice. She was a virgin, but had no scruples about petting if she liked the man. One of the men she had gone with had asked her to marry him. She did not give him an immediate answer, and before she could decide, he decided to marry another woman. He had tried to date her after his marriage, but she had refused to go out with him.

She showed some envy over her younger married sister and declared that younger children had a better opportunity in life. She felt ashamed of the way her parents kept their home—both were somewhat disorganized. Her father was an accountant who had worked for the government for forty years. Her mother had never worked. Mildred visited her parents on Sundays for dinner on an average of once a month.

She spent most of her time with various roommates and was quite active in playing bridge, at tennis and golf, in a play reading group, in a sketching class, and was taking some advanced courses at a graduate school at night, in diverse areas, for "no reason except that I am interested."

Overall, my impression was that Mildred was essentially normal. There was no indication of any serious aberration of any kind. She was a reasonable, practical, efficient, hard-working, active, sensible young woman with considerable sensitivity, reluctant to take chances and highly conservative, with a poor concept of herself as a woman.

My strategy was to try, first of all, to let her come to the conclusion that the cause for her single condition lay in her essentially faulty attitudes toward herself, and for her to assume a more hopeful attitude which would then lead her to make herself more attractive, learn skills to attract men, be ready to ask her roommates to arrange double dates, etc.

Without any direct advice I listened to her and tried to open her mind to consideration of reasons for her present situation. Then, in one session, she said something which led me to use roleplaying right then and there, with rather spectacular consequences, as it turned out.

M: Last Saturday I was playing tennis with one of my roommates and she hit a high ball. I ran, kind of backwards, and right into this man who was playing on the next court. I just fell into his arms and down we both went! We got up, and everybody, including me, laughed. It was one of those naturally funny things, the way it happened. And nobody was hurt. Well, this fellow picked up my racket and he said to me, "How about having a coke after you finish your game?" I told him "No" and he went away.

FIRST ROLEPLAYING

Here was a situation which any therapist could have responded to in any one of many ways. I chose to roleplay and from this point I (T—therapist) and my patient (M—Mildred) will attempt to reenact, in detail, what happened in the office.

T: I'd like to roleplay that situation with you, Mildred.

M: What's that?

T: Let us reenact the situation on the tennis court. I'll play the young man and you play your own part. We'll try to act out the situation as it occurred.

M: Whatever for? What good will that do? It's over and done with.

T: I'll explain later. (I got up and stood next to Mildred.) Please stand up. (She did so.) Now, just make out that you are chasing that ball and hit up against me and we'll fall down.

M: But why? What's the purpose, Doctor?

T: Please humor me for the moment. Just act exactly as you did Saturday.

M: All right. (Mildred began moving backwards in the office, swung her arm, backed into me, and we "fell" on to a couch that I had aimed for.)

T (YM): (Therapist acting the role of the young man.) Oophs.

M (M): (Mildred acting Mildred.) Oh, I *am* sorry.

T (YM): Here, Miss, let me get your tennis racket. I guess I didn't see you coming.

M (M): I guess it was my fault. I did so want to get that ball. I am so sorry I knocked you down.

T (YM): Well, it sure was funny how we spilled over like we did. Say, how about having a coke with me after your game?

M (M): No.

T (YM): Why not?

M (M): I can't. After the game I have to hurry home.

T (YM): Oh, all right. Maybe next time if I see you again.

M (M): Maybe.

We sat down and I asked Mildred if the scene had, indeed, gone more or less as we had acted it. She said it did. I then asked her how she felt when I asked her to have a drink with me and she said "kind of panicked, I guess." On hearing this my immediate strategy was to try to make her socially competent in this situation right then and there. I proposed to do this by repeating this same situation over and over until she reached a satisfactory level of behavior.

T: Mildred, I want to play that scene over again. This time you will be the young man and I will play you. We will change roles. I will try to act just as you did. You will try to act as the young man did. The reasons are severalfold.

You will get a chance to see how you act by watching me imitate you.

You will get a chance to understand the feelings of the young man.

You will get a chance to understand how you interpret the behavior of others in relation to yourself.

Then Mildred, playing the young man [M (YM)], and I, playing Mildred [T (M)], went through the same scene again. After it was over (a matter of two minutes) we sat down, and I asked her for an evaluation.

M: Well, you—I—the part you played of me, was pretty bad.
T: In what way?
M: Well, I seemed *so* gauche, so awkward, almost rude.
T: Why did I—and you—probably reject the young man?
M: I guess I was scared. I just didn't know how to handle myself.
T: Fine. Now, if you please, let us repeat the scene. This time you should try to be competent and you will accept his invitation. Are you willing to try? Same situation. You be you and I'll be the young man.

We replayed the scene and poor Mildred botched it badly. We then reversed our roles and again I played the role of Mildred as I thought she should behave. Then we rehearsed the scene again, and again, and again, from time to time sitting down and analyzing her performance. Finally, our hour coming to an end, we parted.

Now, before telling the surprising result of this hour, let us go over the principles so far.

1. I felt reasonably sure that Mildred was a well-integrated, firm-minded young woman and could engage in roleplaying with no harm.

2. I wanted to see directly by action, rather than indirectly by narrative, how she behaved in such a situation (which was one reason for our initial roleplaying).

3. I felt that if she were to repeat her behavior of the prior Saturday in the freedom of my office that she would get some insight into her behavior.

4. I felt that if we would then reverse roles and I would play her as she had played herself, that she would gain some further understanding of how others saw her (outsight), and some understanding of the feelings of the young man (empathy), and some understanding of how she thought others felt about her (idiopanima).

5. Through my playing her role in a more competent manner, I would give her some kind of a model to imitate.

6. Finally, I felt that if she could play that scene in a competent manner, even in the artificial situation of an office with her therapist, she would get valuable social practice, which would have veridicality, or psychological validity, and might become incorporated into her life style.

When she returned for her next interview, her first words were: "I have had three dates, with three men, since I last saw you!"

It seemed that she went back to the same tennis court and within several hours talked to at least a dozen men, on various pretexts, and emerged from that court with three dates. She ticked them off for me.

"I went to a movie that night with Tom. He's working as a salesman in a store. Sunday I went for a ride with Dick. He's a clerk working for a newspaper. And last night I went to a concert with Harry. He's a dentist."

For several more weeks we discussed all kinds of things, including Dick, the man she was now dating steady. We had many points to cover: whether or not she should introduce Dick to her parents, and when she did so she was able, probably because of our discussions, to behave in a fairly relaxed manner. The romance went along in a rather limping manner and one day she offered the information that Dick had been previously married and that he had informed her that he had no intention of marrying again until he completed his education (he was studying to become a high school teacher) which would take another three years.

Mildred was unwilling to date anyone else while going with Dick and she did not want to give him up. Because I felt that these attitudes had to do with her value system (A good girl does not date seriously with more than one man at a time;

I like Dick and I think we are good for one another), I made no attempt to change her attitudes.

Mildred and Dick saw each other regularly twice a week; they petted rather heavily and she was a bit concerned about his evident desire for sexual intercourse. She began to consider dropping him and began to feel that she was a failure because he would not ask her to marry him. I saw an opportunity for some more roleplaying after this interchange between Mildred and myself.

T: You think Dick is the man for you?

M: Yes, he's a very fine person and has high standards. But I can't go on like this. We see each other twice a week and I know he wants sex. But I see no future in that. I don't want to use sex as a weapon but I won't go to bed with him. Not that he's asked me but I know that's what he wants.

T: Do you think that marriage with you is the right thing for *him?*

M: Yes, it is. He had this disastrous short marriage. This other girl was from a well-to-do family and she left him because he couldn't afford to keep her in the style she wanted. I can help him finish school; I can work while he goes to school full time. I would be just what he needs but the poor goose is just too careful and he does not want to make another mistake.

T: Why don't you have it out with him and tell him you want him to marry you? If he has no intentions to marry, break off and find another more suitable man.

M: I've thought of that, but I love him. I don't want to give him up. I won't find a nicer person.

T: Well, you have several choices. You can keep seeing him and just wait. You can drop him and find another. You can get him to marry you.

M: How can I get him to ask me to marry him?

T: Why not tell him your situation as frankly as you can?

M: I can't do that. Besides, there are three things that bother me and I don't know if he would marry me if he knew them.

T: Three things? What are they?

M: Well, first, I earn more than he does. He doesn't know what I earn and I think if he finds out that this will make him feel more inferior and not want to marry me.

T: The second reason?

M: I'm older than he. He's twenty-nine, and I'm thirty-three. I'm sure he thinks I'm his age or younger than he is.

T: And the third reason?

M: Well, I hope you'll understand. I'm coming to you. Suppose he learns that I'm in therapy. What will he think of me?

SECOND ROLEPLAYING

I saw at this point another chance to meet this problem by means of roleplaying, and once again saw no reason, except possibly not being fair to a bachelor, for not breaking the impasse. I suggested that we roleplay a scene and she agreed.

We sat on a couch, I at her left side, and I said, "We're in the car. I'm Dick, and you're Mildred. I'll park by the road to look at the moon, and let us see how your conversation with Dick could go."

T(D): Say, Mildred, a full moon. Isn't it beautiful? Have you noticed how large the moon looks when it's close to the horizon?

M(M): Yes, it is nice. How did it go at the office today?

T(D): Same as always. I find the work so dull. I can't wait until I have my degree. I'm finding history quite difficult. There is so much reading to do.

M(M): That's too bad. I never liked history myself.

T(D): Well, how are you today? You seem kind of quiet.

M(M): Well, it was a tough day for me, too.

T(D): Anything on your mind?

M(M): No, nothing.

T: Well, let us change seats. You be Dick and I'll be you. Start off with the line about the moon.

M(D): Isn't that a beautiful moon?

T(M): Dick, I have something important to say to you.

M(D): What's that?

T(M): Dick, I am concerned about us. I'm thirty-three years old. I like you very much and I'm not dating anyone else. You told me you didn't want to get married until you get a better job. Well, I want to get married. You know that, don't you?

M(D): Yes, I know that. But you know I can't. I have to finish school first. I can't support a wife.

T(M): Dick, do you know I earn more than you? I could help you finish school sooner if we got married.

M(D): No. I will not be supported by a wife.

T(M): I have something else to tell you and I hope you'll not be shocked. I am seeing a psychologist.

M(D): What's wrong with you?

Not to drag this out, we can summarize this session by saying that once again Mildred and I changed roles several times. Bit by bit, while roleplaying, she was able to mention her age, her earnings, and the fact that she was in therapy.

When she returned for her next session she was engaged to be married. But what was funny, no other word for it, was how the real encounter went. As told by Mildred, this was the essence of the interchange.

M: I think we ought to have an understanding, Dick.

D: About getting married?

M: How did you know?

D: Well, I suppose that's all that's in your mind. I've been talking it over with my therapist and . . .

M: Your therapist? You're in therapy?

D: What's so shocking about that? I've been asking him whether I should marry you and he doesn't think I'm ready yet.

M: I'm going to a therapist, too.

D: Lots of people are. So, he doesn't think I'm ready.

M: Do you know that I am older than you are?

D: I figure you're about thirty-five or so. I think marriages to older women work out better. They are more sensible.

M: Do you know what I earn?

D: I suppose about seven-hundred dollars a month.

M: Well, almost that, not quite. How do you feel about it?

D: Well, as I told my therapist, if we did get married, I could possibly go to school days and could finish up sooner, and then if you have a baby after I'm working, you can stop working.

M: Let's get married, Dick. We don't have to listen to any therapist.

D: Mildred, I've been giving the matter a lot of thought. I don't know if the marriage will be good for you but you're the best thing that ever happened to me. You're the kind of girl I need. I want you to meet my mother. She's been suggesting that I marry you whenever I've told her about you.

ANALYSIS

Our purpose is to give an example of the use of roleplaying in helping a person gain social competency.

By roleplaying two crucial scenes in her life, Mildred gained experience, direct and meaningful to her, which enabled her to act in a more competent manner instead of running away in a panic. The roleplaying alone did not affect her whole personality. It must be remembered that the entire therapeutic relationship lasted for some forty sessions, and only two of these involved roleplaying. However, they were timed just right and in each case there was a successful conclusion.

What is the explanation? Looking back, this seems the simple answer. She had successfully met a realistic life test in each of the two situations we played. Consequently, when she experienced the same situation in reality, it was something already in her experience. The veridicality of the roleplaying made the real life test familiar. She gained experience in roleplaying in a situation in which she could not fail. This, added to insights about herself, clarification of her style of life and encouragement due to the therapeutic interviews contributed both to the roleplaying success and the real life situation.

« CHAPTER ELEVEN »

Summary and Conclusions

IN OUR TIME many people (some estimates run as high as one hundred percent) have personal problems of the type that call for outside assistance. Called "emotional," "behavioral," "personality," or "mental," these problems tend to demonstrate themselves by internal discomfort and by inadequate, inappropriate, bizarre, and generally incompetent behavior.

Individuals with such problems generally do two things: they bear them with patient, passive, pessimistic stoicism, or they do something about them. The latter may be in terms of acting out, such as delinquency, or trying to reach solutions in a wide variety of ways: by changing jobs, locations, marriages, by study, prayer, hobbies, reflection, contemplation. In some cases people discuss their problems informally with friends, neighbors, and even strangers, and formally with various professional people with a variety of training, backgrounds, and skills.

This book is an explanation of and an argument for the use of a method of considerable flexibility, whose use does not commit one to any specific theory of personality any more than does the interview. The procedure, known as roleplaying, is a natural method of interaction used by all children in their play. It consists essentially of a formal agreement for a group of people to act "as if" a situation to be enacted were actually occurring. Therapists may employ this procedure in individual and in group therapy for one or any combination of three major purposes: to better understand the patient, to instruct him, or to give him new experiences in behaving.

The value of this method depends on three major interlocking elements: the immediate utilization, usually at exaggerated levels, of feelings, emotions, and behavior; the tendency for the individual to creatively experiment with new solutions in the safe atmosphere of therapy; and the creation of a veridical situation which becomes psychologically valid for the patient.

Roleplaying has numerous variations and formats. The basic ones have been described in the book proper and some others are defined in the glossary or are mentioned in the annotated bibliography. Therapists who use roleplaying generally design or adapt various formats to meet individual needs.

The argument for employing roleplaying is that it is a neutral form of interaction, relatively theory-free in its essence; that for some purposes it is ideal, such as getting to see and hear how a person really operates rather than geting information through narration; it can be used to show a person, rather than only to tell him, how he acts or should act; and it can give the patient realistic rather than symbolic experience in new behavior.

While the writer, in his general practice in individual or group psychotherapy, has his patients roleplay about ten percent of the time he is with them, perhaps other therapists may utilize roleplaying one percent of the time; others may use it up to fifty percent. In any case, the method is not a total substitute for either the interview or other procedures.

The most basic philosophic argument here developed is that all procedures, regardless of their history, who developed them, or who uses them, should be considered common property. Insidious remarks about the "couch" or about "hypnosis" or "finger painting" should have no place in the language of mature therapists. The therapist who is tied to any single technique, unless it be for research purposes, is doing himself and his patient a disservice.

Roleplaying appears to be an effective and therefore an economical method of operating. Since the major social problem in psychotherapy is that of meeting the needs of so many people with a limited number of professional workers, experimentation with procedures that are faster or cheaper for particular purposes seems to be a professional obligation.

Just reading this book, which attempts to answer with brevity the major questions asked by students, does not automatically make the reader capable of using this technique. He must now roleplay in reality (the sociological definition), and thus learn to employ the method by practice. To repeat an earlier caution: work by easy stages, handle simple problems in simple ways, do a little at a time, and wait for results.

Annotated Bibliography

IN PLANNING *Roleplaying in Psychotherapy,* one of the problems was integrating the considerable literature in this field. Since it was hoped to present a volume that would not only present a single overall position, but also one that would take due cognizance of other peoples' opinions and experiences, our decision was to attempt to summarize the literature in an independent, annotated bibliography.

Practically the entire known periodical literature was read, and all articles which had some kind of theoretical or procedural content, in contrast to recital of cases alone, were abstracted, following the language of the various authors when possible. To the writer's best knowledge, these one hundred thirty-three abstracts represent more than half of the total literature in this field.

This section is intended to be read as a separate and independent chapter of the book. It should complement Dr. Corsini's presentation and give the reader a sense of current opinions and findings about therapeutic roleplaying.

SAMUEL S. CARDONE

1. ABLESSER, H. "Role reversal" in a group psychotherapy session. *Group Psychotherapy,* 1962, 15, 321-325.

Group psychotherapy with four boys arrested for separate auto thefts is recounted. Each boy was asked to place himself in the role of a car owner and to express how he would feel if *his* car had been stolen. All four agreed they would be angry and would want the auto thief to be punished. The author suggested they place themselves in the roles of any person they might think of hurting.

2. ACKERMAN, M. & ACKERMAN, SYLVIA. Emergency psychodrama for an acute psychosomatic syndrome. *Group Psychotherapy* 1962, 15, 84-88.

A one-session episode illustrates how various psychodramatic techniques were used to alleviate psychosomatic symptoms developed under conflict. Varying techniques were used in rapid sequence to prevent the patient from mobilizing resistance.

3. BACH, G. R. Dramatic play therapy with adult groups. *Journal of Psychology,* 1950, 29, 225-246.

The play drama, a group therapy technique for disturbed adults, was developed to enable the psychotherapist to bring projective fantasies under therapeutic management. Its inherently non-directive characteristics distinguish it from psychodrama. Three processes are hypothesized as being facilitated by the technique: 1. fosters interdependence between members of psychotherapy groups; 2. instigates a symbolic learning process resulting in greater objectivity in the perception of the self role in living reality; 3. facilitates relatively uninhibited communication of tabu feelings. Protocols, research, and case findings seem to support these hypotheses.

4. BAXTER, W. A. Psychodramatic experience within a religious setting. *Group Psychotherapy,* 1960, 13, 40-46.

One hundred and seven adolescents participated in a week long conference on religious living. This article deals primarily with the roleplaying aspects of the conference. A roleplay drama, was acted out for the first three days for two one-hour periods. The conferees generally agreed that the roleplaying provided them with a better understanding of themselves and others.

5. Blake, R. R. Experimental psychodrama with children. *Group Psychotherapy,* 1955, 8, 347-350.

In roleplaying in the home the psychodramatic theater is the house, the players are the child and his parents. The scenes are everyday, ordinary ones such as working out a conflict or giving instruction of the kind occurring during socialization. The goals are to quicken social learning, to further systematic knowledge of socialization, to increase spontaneous reactions and to have fun. Blake feels psychodrama: 1. makes it possible to sense the child's world; 2. develops the child's sensitivity by helping him see and experience the world from many different views; and 3. hastens the learning of new social skills.

6. Bobroff, A. J. Religious psychodrama. *Group Psychotherapy,* 1963, 16, 37-38.

Religious psychodrama deals with personal problems associated with religious feelings. A characteristic session is presented in which a woman asked the question, "Why doesn't God answer people's prayers?" The director obtained a specific instance and set up a psychodramatic scene. Role reversal and other psychodramatic techniques were used followed by a group discussion.

7. Boring, R. O. & Deabler, H. L. A simplified psychodramatic approach in group therapy. *Journal of Clinical Psychology,* 1951, 7, 371-375.

Simplified psychodrama does not require a stage. Besides the director-therapist, two persons are needed to play male and female auxiliary roles. Occasionally auxiliary roles may be played by patients themselves. The authors present structured situations they have developed around basic problem areas more or less common to all patients. Group discussions initiated and stimulated by the director of the group follow the session. Simplified psychodrama: 1. provides an opportunity for patients to work through unresolved problems and conflicts; 2. provides an opportunity for patients to share their private world with others; 3. presents a unique learning opportunity; 4. brings an awareness of the commonality of problems and life situations; 5. is a bridge between hospital and outside world adjustment.

8. Bour, P. Psychodrama in a psychiatric hospital in France. *Group Psychotherapy,* 1962, 15, 305-311.

   Psychodrama appears especially valuable with schizophrenic patients, allowing a means of communication as well as providing the therapist with diagnostic information.

9. Brandzel, Rose. Role playing as a training device in preparing multiple-handicapped youth for employment. *Group Psychotherapy,* 1963, 16, 16-21.

   Roleplaying is an effective method of preparing youths to get and hold jobs. Opportunities are provided by this method for gaining missing life experiences. Practice for requirements and demands on job situations is obtained. Roleplaying helps to establish adequate behavior patterns and verbal responses. In addition, this procedure helps to develop personal confidence and competence.

10. Bromberg, W. Acting and acting out. *American Journal of Psychotherapy*, 1958, 12, 264-268.

    Acting-out is discouraged in psychoanalytic treatment because it represents resistance to recovery of unconscious memories in the transference relationship. On the other hand, acting and acting-out are integral parts of psychodrama. Bromberg speculates that activity, by which is meant both acting and acting out, as it occurs in psychodrama, comes closer to the motive value of object-words representing original emotional experience than verbal interpretations of behavior. thus pointing to a need for an increase of action methods in psychotherapy.

11. BROMBERG, W. & FRANKLIN, G. H. The treatment of sexual deviates with group psychodrama. *Group Psychotherapy,* 1952, 4, 274-289.

A program was undertaken at Mendocino State Hospital involving seventy-five patients convicted of sexual offenses, ranging from incest to lewd and lascivious conduct. A sequential description of the eighty-one sessions, dividing the program into four phases is given. In the early phase, or warming up period, anxieties emerged. The middle phase was dominated by the emergence of dependency reactions. The next phase, which began at approximately the sixty-third session, was characterized by an increase of acting-out behavior and more portrayals of individual problems. The seventy-sixth session marked the beginning of the final phase, in which ambivalent feelings and finally, reality appreciation, prevailed.

12. BRUCK, M. An example of the use of psychodrama in the relieving of an acute symptom in a psychiatric children's clinic. *Group Psychotherapy,* 1954, 6, 216-221.

A case study of an eight and one-half year old boy with tics and a partial paralysis of his upper right arm is presented. Symptoms appeared almost immediately following a vaccination. To achieve the goals of anxiety and tension relief, psychodrama was selected because of its facility 1. for making a quick supportive relationship, and 2. discharge of tension. When the patient was sufficiently warmed up, roleplaying and role-reversal techniques were employed to reenact the vaccination. Finally, the patient roleplayed the traumatic scene. This appeared to allow patient to discharge many of his accumulated tensions and fears as they related to the specific traumatic experience. The tic and partial paralysis disappeared. An eighteen month follow-up indicated patient continued to be symptom free as well as reverting to his normal pre-vaccination behavior.

13. BUCK, BETSY. Psychodrama of drug addiction. *Group Psychotherapy,* 1952, 4, 301-321.

Buck presents a transcript of a psychodrama session conducted by J. L. Moreno with a drug addict, other addicts serving as auxiliary egos. The therapist brings the group discussion from the specific to the general, from individual problems to consideration of the society in which these problems were born and to which the members will return.

14. BUTTS, W. M. Psychodrama with students and their wives. *Group Psychotherapy,* 1962, 15, 55-57.

Patients tend to discuss sexual problems in individual therapy, but not during group psychodrama. Role identification and rebellion against authority are discussed in both settings. Although there were some positive results of the psychodrama sessions, they were not of great therapeutic value. Patients tended to be less restricted, interacted more at the feeling level, and more willingly discussed their problems than students and wives.

15. CARP, E. A. D. E. Psychodrama. *Z. Psychotherapie Medical Psychologie,* 1954, 4, 163-170.

Through psychodrama the individual is able to perceive the less personal, more social aspects of his problems; his guilt is lessened and his perspective is increased through objectification of feelings. In degree of spontaneity, psychodrama seems intermediate between natural child play and psychoanalytic play techniques. It is of particular value in preparing a person for individual psychotherapy.

16. CARTENSON, B. The auxiliary chair technique. *Group Psychotherapy,* 1955, 8, 50-56.

Short term roleplaying was employed in a research program to help change the behavior of rejected or "left out" children. The procedure included sociometric and observational data which served for planning the first one-hour therapeutic session. A second observation, plus the report of the first session of roleplaying, served for planning the second session. Sociometric measurements and observations were used to measure change. A chair was used in the place of an auxiliary ego. The two roleplaying sessions included the following sequential steps: 1. introducing the game and discovering safe areas; 2. eliciting feelings behind behavior; 3. discovering causes of behavior; 4. determining how others feel about the behavior; 5. helping others change behavior; 6. changing own behavior; and 7. intention setting.

17. CORSINI, R. J. The method of psychodrama in prison. *Group Psychotherapy,* 1951, 3, 321-326.

Three basic steps in organizing psychodrama in a prison are: 1. the formation of effective transference with natural leaders; 2. the formation of a core; 3. the addition of new members to the core group. Early sessions should be spent in general theoretical discussion, mutual introductions, roleplaying and sociodrama, for the purpose of enabling members to know one another better. Complete freedom to leave the group exists, and periodic weeding out, either by the group as a whole or by the therapist must be done to eliminate those who will not participate, those who are so maladjusted as to threaten the group, and all those who are unadaptable. Preliminary sessions approach open-confessional methods of the Oxford movement. Following four or five preliminary sessions, the director explains the purpose of psychodrama and how to participate in it. Psychodrama is an effective psychotherapeutic approach in a penal institution, since it penetrates surface feelings, difficult to accomplish with other techniques in this setting.

18. CORSINI, R. J. Psychodramatic treatment of a pedophile. *Group Psychotherapy,* 1951, 4, 166-171.

This is a case study of a prisoner participating in a psychodrama group at San Quentin Prison. The location of what appeared to be the source of the subject's difficulties was determined during the fifth reenactment of the same scene involving the subject and his father, in which the relationship that existed between them began to become apparent to the subject and other group members. The subject subsequently associated the crime with hidden feelings he had toward his father. The psychodramatic techniques employed appeared to facilitate overt expression of hostility toward the father which had the subsequent effect of producing insight.

19. CORSINI, R. J. Immediate therapy. *Group Psychotherapy,* 1952, 4, 322-330.

Since psychodrama is quick and cheap, it is of greater social value than psychoanalysis. In conducting psychodrama, one is doing individual therapy in a group situation, which involves establishing a common bond of understanding and self-direction of the subject. The therapist should strive to achieve a peak of emotional effect, within the subject's limit of tolerance but beyond the threshold of control. Some therapeutic principles are: attempt rapid therapy, precipitate anxiety and then refuse to reduce it. Solutions irradiate to various areas, in terms of goal direction.

20. CORSINI, R. J. The "behind your back" technique in group psychotherapy and psychodrama. *Group Psychotherapy,* 1953, 6, 102-109.

Group therapy should be natural in form. The natural way for a group of people to discuss an individual is to gossip "behind his back." If a gossip group discusses an individual, and the individual discussed overhears the conversation this would be a natural means of human interaction for therapeutic purposes. The "behind the back" method goes as follows: A subject volunteers. He discusses any problem, speaking about ten to thirty minutes. The subject then "goes out of the room" psychologically but not physically by retreating behind a screen, or by simply turning his back to the group. Each member of the group is urged by the therapist to make a comment about the "absent" member, and a discussion develops. The subject later "returns" for further discussion.

21. CORSINI, R. J. Psychodrama with a psychopath. *Group Psychotherapy,* 1958, 11, 33-39.

A training school inmate who was diagnosed as a "primary psychopath," escaped and stole a car. Pursued by the police, he crashed, but was uninjured. When the subject returned to the therapeutic group, a psychodramatic session which consisted of four scenes in which the subject "crashed," "was killed," "his body identified by his parents," and "burial" took place. No post discussion occurred. A follow-up showed a remarkable, beneficial behavioral change. Psychodrama appears to be an effective means of communicating messages to individuals diagnosed "psychopath," enabling such individuals to attain an emotional understanding of their problems.

22. DREWS, R. S. Psychodrama in private practice. *Group Psychotherapy,* 1952, 5, 70-72.

A patient with "writer's cramps" had been in various forms of psychotherapy; psychoanalysis, medical, and osteopathic treatment. Each of these methods was ineffective. The patient, a court clerk for the past twenty years, had been dealing with the same judge. Through the use of role reversal, the patient was able to see how he viewed the judge, his reactions to this individual, and his position as court clerk. His "writer's cramp" disappeared during the psychodrama session. Follow up indicated no recurrence of the symptom. The patient also reported a more satisfying relationship with the judge.

23. ELIASOPH, E. A group therapy and psychodrama approach with adolescent drug addicts. *Group Psychotherapy,* 1955, 8, 161-167.

The value of group psychotherapy with drug addicts is discussed with excerpts of some sessions. Psychodramatic techniques enable the therapist to get fuller expression of feelings, attitudes toward self, toward others, toward treatment, and encourage freer interaction between group members. Psychodrama proved beneficial in enabling addicts to gain greater awareness of distortions and expectations in interpersonal relationships. The therapist assigned roles to members in situations ranging from interplay between mother and patient in various anxiety-provoking situations, to negotiations with a "pusher" when looking for drugs, to attitudes and feelings when taking drugs.

24. ELIASOPH, E. Concepts and techniques of roleplaying and role training utilizing psychodramatic methods in group therapy with adolescent drug addicts. *Group Psychotherapy,* 1955, 8, 308-315.

Roleplaying, to accomplish the goal of helping drug addicts, is discussed. The author concludes that role training techniques in group therapy have proven effective in reproducing the sense of urgency and reality of the real life situation. Individual therapy has proven insufficient in handling drug addicts.

25. ELIASOPH, E. A group therapy–psychodrama program at Berkshire Industrial Farm. *Group Psychotherapy,* 1958, 11, 57-62.

At the Berkshire Industrial Farm, a group psychotherapy–psychodrama program has been used for one and one-half years. This program has proved effective in: 1. socializing isolated individuals; 2. facilitating expression of feelings; 3. giving boys an opportunity to learn what the other fellow is thinking about; 4. affording youngsters an opportunity to test the reactions of adults, and to relate to them in a permissive, nonthreatening atmosphere; 5. facilitating staff understanding and rapport; 6. establishing greater, "esprit de corps" in the total institutional setting.

26. ENNEIS, J. M. A note on the organization of the St. Elizabeth's Hospital psychodrama program. *Group Psychotherapy,* 1951, 3, 253-255.

The patient program divides itself into four major sections: 1. the acute group, 2. continued therapy groups (sick from 5-35 years), 3. sex psychopaths, 4. patients ready to be discharged. Emphasis is placed on attitudes to be met in the family, job, social, and community settings. Role practice and training are used as indicated. In groups where the parents, who are invited, do not attend, auxiliary egos are used. Enneis also discusses a psychodrama training program for the staff.

27. ENNEIS, J. M. Establishing a psychodrama program. *Group Psychotherapy,* 1952, 5, 111-119.

Job descriptions of the psychodramatist, assistant to the psychodramatist, and psychodrama technician are given, as well as details of a psychodrama theater including measurements, surroundings, stage lighting, furniture and seating. In selecting patients, diagnosis is of no consequence. It is important to have a favorable sociometric structure into which the patient may fit. Recording equipment is advisable.

28. FANTEL, E. Psychodrama in a veteran's hospital. *Sociatry,* 1948, 2, 47-64.

Psychodrama was used with ex-servicemen patients who shared a specific problem—anticipated difficulty with their wives or fiancees. Each session was devoted to the problem of one patient, while the others listened or acted as auxiliary egos.

29. FANTEL, E. Report on psychodramatic therapy. *Group Psychotherapy,* 1950, 3, 55-58.

Psychodrama has been used: 1. to complement insulin and electric therapy; 2. in facilitating understanding between patients and their relatives; 3. as a training device for psychiatric attendants; 4. in combination with the *Make a Picture Story Test (MAPS).*

30. FANTEL, E. Psychodrama in an Army General Hospital. *Group Psychotherapy,* 1952, 4, 290-300.

Several psychodrama scenes with a hospitalized soldier typical of many cases handled in an Army General Hospital are reported. Fantel believes that psychodrama brings into focus underlying personality problems of the patient, enabling him to see himself as others see him, and to understand that self. Psychodrama provides patients with opportunities to air suppressed resentments as well as build up self esteem. Psychodrama enables the group to share a mass kindness and understanding that makes possible a gradual progression toward adjustment. By psychodramatic rehearsal of "future scenes" that the patients would meet upon return to society, possibility of a relapse was minimized. Psychodrama is a practicable method of handling war neuroses and of quickly returning men to service or civilian life.

31. FEIN, LEAH G. Psychodrama in the treatment of disciplinary problems. *Group Psychotherapy*, 1962, 15, 147-153.

In disciplinary situations where the rules broken cannot be defined with precision, where infringements involve emotions, attitudes, and value systems, roleplaying is a valuable tool. Many different feelings, attitudes, and value systems can be played out in the open so that all participants get a clear view of the dynamics of the individuals involved. A case study illustrates the use of psychodramatic techniques when a teacher is faced with a disciplinary problem.

32. FEIN, LEAH, G. The use of psychodrama to strengthen self-concepts of student nurses. *Group Psychotherapy*, 1963, 16, 161-163.

Student nurses were having difficulty relating to the children, parents of children, and nurses' aides, being either too dogmatic. controlling or permissive. In addition, the studients generally griped and complained about everything and everyone. Fein felt that students were uncertain and anxious about their roles, status, and responsibilities, which led them into defensive behaviors that resulted in ineffectual ward functioning. A group dynamics program was initiated which was held for one hour each week to help the students clarify their identities and roles, become more aware of their feelings and learn how to handle these feelings constructively. Interpersonal conflict situations were illustrated through sociodrama. Intrapersonal conflicts were treated by psychodrama. The general consensus of the hospital staff was that the students rapidly improved in relationships with patients, parents of patients and with co-workers. A summary of common problems peculiar to student nurses that emerged from these sessions is offered.

33. FINK, A. K. The case for the "open" psychodramatic session. A dialogue. *Group Psychotherapy*, 1960, 94-100.

Fink raises questions concerning public psychodramatic sessions. Does the lack of confidentiality afforded the protagonist in an open psychodramatic session violate professional ethics? Fink states it is ethically necessary for participants to be properly oriented and allowed freedom of choice to participate. Despite the director's control, the subject may reveal more personal material than intended. This is a risk always involved in psychodrama. For subjects who disclose problems which require more treatment than a single session, an open session serves as an impetus to seek further treatment.

34. Fink, A. K. The democratic essence of psychodrama. *Group Psychotherapy,* 1963, 16, 156-160.

Basic to democracy is respect for the worth and dignity of individuals and groups. In roleplaying, the director, as a democratic leader, facilitates the process by which the group locates, explores, and then attempts to resolve problems.

35. Godenne, Ghislaine D. Outpatient adolescent group psychotherapy. II. Use of co-therapists, psychodrama, and parent group therapy. *American Journal of Psychotherapy,* 1965, 19(1), 40-53.

On the basis of observations made with four outpatient adolescent groups, Godenne suggests: 1. compatible co-therapists (male and female), with one assuming the leading role; 2. a parent group to be run simultaneously with the adolescent group but using a different therapist; 3. group meetings to last no more than one hour; 4. members of the group should include both sexes and may fall into a variety of diagnostic classifications; 5. group members should be at the same level of maturity; 6. the group should be labeled a psychotherapy group and no attempt be made to mask this fact; 7. each member should be carefully evaluated to determine the advantage of group therapy versus individual therapy. Psychodrama is a useful tool in adolescent group therapy, providing a means for the adolescent to tell the group what is going on at home or at school without revealing the "secrets" of his life; consequently, he has less need to build up defenses against talking about the problems he is facing. Psychodrama, to some degree has the status of a game in which the patient is allowed to describe situations in a pseudo-real setting, but to express real feelings. It also adds, through the motor activity so inherent in adolescence, a useful tool of communication. Psychodrama should be introduced in the first meeting.

36. GOODMAN, J. M. Nondirective psychodramatic play therapy. *American Journal of Orthopsychiatry,* 1962, 32, 532-534.

Nondirective play therapy is a composite of play therapy and psychodrama, employed according to the principles of nondirective therapy. It is designed to: 1. function as a catalyst to expedite emotional catharsis; 2. reveal dynamic material; 3. serve as a diagnostic tool; and 4. reduce threat to the youngster. The therapist serves as the director. His function is to reflect the feelings of the dolls which are in action.

37. GREENBERG, I. Audience in action through psychodrama. *Group Psychotherapy,* 1964, 17, 104-122.

Psychodrama is seen as a means of bringing psychotherapy to those for whom it might not otherwise be available and achieving this goal through placing emphasis on a large audience toward which therapy would be directed.

38. GREENBERGER, P. A reaction to an experience, the psychodrama. *Group Psychotherapy,* 1963, 16, 250-254.

Of the psychodramatic methods, Greenberger feels role reversal and spontaneous improvisations are particularly helpful. Psychodramatic techniques lead to immediate results.

39. GREENHILL, M. Psycho-dramatic play therapy in disorders of childhood. *Proceedings, Institute of Child Research, Woods Schools,* 1945. 12, 107-122.

Greenhill handled fourteen children with psychodramatic play therapy. Reasonably good results were obtained in the case of six children. The method was not used therapeutically with the remaining eight but rather as a means of eliciting material helpful in making recommendations as to the ultimate disposition of the children.

40. GROENEVELD, B. *Spel als Levensspiegel.* (Play as a mirror of life.) Purmerend, Netherlands: J. Muusses, 1957.

A discussion of the procedures of "creative play," a form of roleplaying which has a strong similarity to psychodrama.

41. GUNN, R. L., NAVRAN, D. S. & JERDEN, L. The live presentation of dramatic scenes as a stimulus to patient interaction in group psychotherapy. *Group Psychotherapy,* 1963, 16, 164-172.

Four on-going therapy groups in a VA hospital were exposed to live dramatic scenes dealing with interpersonal conflicts in family life taken from current plays. The patients' diagnoses included character disorders and functional psychoses ranging in severity from substantial remission to openly delusional states. The experimental design was controlled for sex, degree of illness, and the time interval between the presentation of the scenes and the occurrence of the group meetings. The authors hypothesized that viewing the scenes might deepen the level of interaction in the group. There were no significant differences noted between male and female groups, acute and chronic patient groups, and group meetings right after scene presentation and those meeting at a later time; consequently, the hypothesis was not supported by the data. Individual patient reactions are discussed as well as the feelings of the actors participating in the scenes.

42. HAAS, R. B. *Roleplaying and guidance.* 16mm. motion picture film, black and white, sound, 14 min., 1953. Department of Visual Instruction, University of California extension, Berkeley, California.

The use of the roleplaying technique as a help in solving life problems experienced by a young boy is demonstrated. The film shows the boy playing in turn the role of his mother, the role of a school principal, and his own role. Roleplaying brings to the fore basic emotional problems and allows insight into the situation that created the conflict. It helps the subject and his advisor. The film demonstrates the usefulness and the ease with which roleplaying can be used in various school situations.

43. HARROW, GERTRUDE. The effects of psychodrama group therapy on role behavior of schizophrenic patients. *Group Psychotherapy,* 1951, 3, 316-320.

This study derives from the theoretical position that 1. ability to take roles is essential for the development of the "social self," which in turn, plays an important part in adjustment; 2. schizophrenia can be considered due to an inadequately developed "social self" and inability to take roles and share thinking and feeling with others; 3. the schizophrenic's mode of communication tends to be simple, concrete and private. Harrow postulated that psychodrama might be effective in increasing ability to communicate with others and would provide for social and emotional growth. Psychodramatic treatment groups were conducted in the same manner by the same therapist. Two groups of ten schizophrenics each met twenty-five times for a two month period. A control group did not receive any therapy. On the basis of testing and evaluations Harrow concluded that: 1. psychodrama appears to be effective in enhancing the role-taking ability of schizophrenic patients; 2. psychodrama may affect fundamental personality processes as well as overt role-taking behavior; 3. psychodrama leads to personality integration and a gradual "working-through" of problems; 4. psychodrama is particularly well suited for individuals with extreme difficulties in social communication and reality orientation; 5. development of role-taking ability involves a favorable emotional atmosphere, a spontaneous co-learning process and the actual activity of taking the role of another person.

44. HARROW, GERTRUDE S. & HAAS, R. B. Psychodrama in the guidance clinic. *Sociatry*, 1947, 1, 70-81.

Roleplaying situations were presented to a group of guidance workers, using a case history as a base. Nine conflict situations were chosen for enactment. Volunteers acted various roles from the case history.

Discussion of the possible uses of roleplaying techniques in the guidance field followed. The consensus of comments was: 1. roleplaying gives the caseworker insight into the client's personality dynamics; 2. it reveals sharply and quickly the attitudes toward others and one can discover what the client believes the attitude of others to be towards him; 3. roleplaying provides a double clarification process: the client works out his own insights and at the same time reveals disturbing conflicts. Roleplaying has therapeutic and cathartic power. It can be used for 1. exploration, to gain a refinement of the case history; 2. diagnosis; and 3. retraining.

45. HASKELL, M. R. Psychodramatic role training in preparation for release on parole. *Group Psychotherapy,* 1957, 10, 51-59.

Sixty-six inmates being considered for parole were equally divided into an experimental and control group. The experimental group received fifteen role training sessions, each approximately one hour and forty minutes long. Each subject participated at least once in each of three major role clusters. These were occupational roles, family roles, and community roles. Techniques used were self-presentation, soliloquy, projection, role-reversal, double, and mirror. Results indicated a statistically significant difference only between groups with respect to the post-treatment role test.

46. HASKELL, M. R. Group psychotherapy and psychodrama in prison. *Group Psychotherapy,* 1960, 13, 22-33.

Problems peculiar to correctional institutions in utilizing psychodrama, sociodrama, spontaneity training and role training are discussed. Techniques are illustrated to show their value and application. Results indicate that the group receiving role training improved in role playing ability and showed greater conformity to social values, compared with a control group.

47. HERRIOTT, FRANCES. Psychodrama. In T. Muller (Ed.), *Mental health in nursing.* Washington, D.C.: Catholic University of America Press, 1949, Pp. 19-30.

The report of a psychodrama project at St. Elizabeth's Hospital using the classical Moreno techniques. Problems dealt with were those of content, personality difficulties, occupation, adjustment in preparation for leaving the hospital, and social and family relations. Typical sessions are summarized and evaluated.

48. HOFFMAN, J. J. Psychodrama with in-patients. *Group Psychotherapy,* 1961, 14, 186-189.

Psychodrama tends to elicit from the protagonist and the non-protagonist participants a relatively high level of emotional involvement. The special merits of psychodrama are: 1. the emotional impact of the auxiliary ego; 2. role training; 3. the ability to be spontaneous which gives the person a feeling he can conquer his problems.

49. HOLLISTER, W. G. & HUSBAND, G. W. Two roleplaying methods of using mental health films and plays. *Mental Health,* 1955, 39, 277-283.

Two methods involving audiences in roleplaying to be used as a basis for better understanding of principles of mental health are discussed. These methods are employed with the viewing of a film or play. In the "feeling with" method, the director paints a verbal picture of the setting and gives names of the characters. The audience is then invited to share the forthcoming experience of these actors by "living the experience with them." The director forms the audience into subgroups to identify with the principal characters. The film or play is then presented. This is followed by a "buzz session," in which members of each subgroup assemble to discuss their feelings about the role, an interviewing phase, an interaction phase, and a summarization phase. In the "helping group" technique, the audience is told the film will be cut at the point where one individual is giving advice to a distraught individual. At this stage, one member of the audience assumes the role of the distraught mother and the audience assumes the role of the helping individual. This procedure produces a better understanding of individual feelings.

50. KELLY, J. G., BLAKE, R. R., & STROMBERG, C. E. The effect of role training on role reversal. *Group Psychotherapy,* 1957, 10, 95-104.

The authors tested the hypothesis that after role-playing, ascendant subjects will show greater skill in taking submissive roles and conversely, submissive subjects will demonstrate greater skill in taking ascendant roles. Six "submissive" subjects with role training experience showed a significant difference in their responses to the *Allport A-S Reaction Study* when acting "as if" compared to control subjects. Submissive people with role training experience showed a significant difference in ability to resist group pressure in a simulated group situation compared to submissive subjects without such training. Ascendant subjects, however, showed no difference in their responses. The basic assumption that roleplaying increases role-taking skills was partially substantiated.

51. KIELHOLZ, A. VON DER. *Besserung eines Verbrecherischen Geisteskranken* (Improvement in a psychotic criminal.) *Psychology Berater Gesunde Lebensgestalt,* 1952, 4, 430-434.

A case history is presented of an individual who was institutionalized as criminally insane and who improved dramatically after playing the role of Gessler in the play, "Wilhelm Tell." The patient's previous criminality was in the nature of a sublimated exhibitionism from which the roleplaying afforded release.

52. KLINE, N. S. Psychodrama for mental hospitals. *Journal of Clinical Psychopathology,* 1947, 8, 817-825.

The purpose of psychodrama is: 1. to raise selected problems, some of which the patient will have to face after discharge; 2. to suggest various solutions to these problems; 3. to provide the patient with an opportunity to work out his own solution; 4. to permit a frank and unbiased criticism of his success or failure in a "safe" environment. Eight psychodramatic situations are outlined in detail to illustrate the fundamental principles of conducting psychodrama.

53. KREITLER, H. & ELBINGER, S. Psychiatric and cultural aspects of the opposition to psychodrama. *Group Psychotherapy*, 1961, 14, 215-220.

The most frequent objections to psychodrama are: 1. subjects who participate in psychodrama know all the time that they are only playing and are not really influenced by the scenes enacted; 2. the strong dynamics of the psychodramatic scene cause sudden eruption of anxiety producing material without the therapist being able to handle the situations as would be possible in an individual or group setting; 3. psychodrama encourages the patient to translate his dangerous impulses into action and thus to act at the most primitive regressive level. The authors respond to these questions. They conclude that modern man, affected by the bewildering abundance of divergent information, is bound to single theories and it is impossible to decide whether spontaneity is today greater or smaller than in the days of more primitive culture.

54. KURLAND, A. A. An evaluation of drama therapy. *Psychiatric Quarterly Supplements*, 1952, 26, 210-299.

Group therapy with schizophrenic patients, through the mechanisms of dramatization, is a potent force in stimulating group dynamics. This is especially true of patients with predominantly affective reactions. This method of therapy increases the therapeutic potential of patients who rejected individual treatment. The author reports a study using the drama technique and concludes that while no patients were cured by this method alone, patients were helped to stabilize themselves as social beings.

55. LASSNER, R. Psychodrama in prison. *Group Psychotherapy*, 1950, 3, 77-91.

In a diagnostic center for male felons, thirty-five men, all free of manifest mental illness or mental deficiency, voluntarily participated in psychodrama, the groups varying in size at various times from four to ten. Prisoners who had for some time participated in the group volunteered as "auxiliary egos." Upon completion of the program, each participant received a letter requesting an evaluation of the program. Of the twenty-nine reached, nineteen replies were received. Statements were classified into nine groups. They were: 1. "started to think," "learned," "gained insight"; 2. saw oneself "as others see one," "faced reality"; 3. parallelism with others problems; 4. beneficial effect of "advice," "suggestions," "constructive criticism by others"; 5. opportunity to talk freely about one's problems; 6. restoration of self-confidence and optimism; 7. other group members, not caring enough, could not be helped; 8. psychodrama should also deal with present problems, as well as past experiences; 9. it should be applied to a wider population and more frequently.

56. LAWLOR, G. W. Role therapy. *Sociatry,* 1947, 1, 51-55.

Lawlor postulates man is composed of two parts: a central core, the "ego," and a periphery, composed of overlapping "roles." The ego contains behavioral release mechanisms, basic behavioral directions. world perception, self-perception, and ego ideal. Roles are patterns exhibited when the person is in a social situation. Conflict arises when a person is not gaining satisfaction from the principal roles he plays and when there is dissonance between the various roles played. Lawlor suggests: 1. education about the nature of roles; 2. training in the playing of roles. As a means of training individuals to play their roles, helping them to gain personal satisfaction and to become socially effective, roleplaying techniques may be used.

57. LEBOVICI, S. Psychodrama as applied to adolescents. *Journal of Child Psychology and Psychiatry,* 1961, 1, 298-305.

Psychodrama as a diagnostic tool with adolescents is discussed. Therapeutic aspects of psychodrama include transference, freedom of verbal and motoric expression and bodily contact, illustratated in a case study. Various psychodramatic techniques which appear to work well with adolescent groups are discussed.

58. Lehmann, L. & Tourlentes, T. The drama workshop. *Mental Hospitals,* 1963, 14(3), 158-162.

The drama workshop avoids the superficiality of production-oriented dramatics and the blunt probing of psychodrama. Concentrating on patients' behavioral difficulties, it uses structured dramatic situations specifically geared to meet symptomatic needs. It does not, however, employ dramatic situations directly involving the personal problems of the patient. The exercise is usually light and humorous. The four dramatic forms used are pantomime, characterization, script reading and role playing. Lehmann and Tourlentes feel that the drama workshop can effect only a limited amount of change, and is not intended to provide insight or to resolve psychic conflicts. When carefully planned, it provides some realistic experiences that may contribute to the patient's total treatment.

59. Lippitt, Rosemary. Psychodrama in the home. *Sociatry,* 1947, 2, 148-165.

Verbatim accounts are given of roleplaying sessions conducted by a mother in daily living with her two children, a five year old boy and a two year old girl. Approximately thirty minutes daily were spent in roleplaying for about six weeks. Topics came through daily experiences of the children. Typical situations were: 1. dealing with a deep-set fear; 2. overcoming an emotional block of long duration; 3. improving social behavior; 4. achieving understanding and acceptance of the physical abnormalities in other children. Because of the child's limited ability to communicate in words, the director must draw problems from the child. Children seem to have quicker insight concerning relationships between roleplaying and everyday reality situations than do adults. Setting up new patterns of social relationships rather than re-educating ineffective established patterns is more profitable. Parental roleplaying seems to make it easy to transfer a warm emotional relationship to other adult-child relationships, such as the teacher-child relationships, outside the home.

60. LIPPITT, ROSEMARY. The auxiliary chair technique. *Group Psychotherapy,* 1958, 11, 8-26.

The auxiliary chair technique substitutes chairs for the subject or auxiliary egos, to attain objective analysis and clarification. This technique is useful as: 1. a natural stepping stone from lectures to roleplaying; 2. to avoid over- or under-playing a role when using it as a teaching technique with novices; 3. for research purposes; 4. to enable the director to portray an episode and then step back to become a co-observer along with the patient; 5. to reduce the cost of several trained auxiliary egos; 6. to add magnification of a specific role; 7. to allow the subject to project; 8. to control depth; 9. to prevent undesirable role identification; 10. to prevent embarrassment to the client when his behavior is mirrored; 11. to reassure overanxious, depressed, or suspicions patients, when an auxiliary ego might prove too much for the patient to face at the moment.

61. LIPPITT, ROSEMARY & HUBBELL, ANNE. Roleplaying for personnel and guidance workers: review of the literature with suggestions for application. *Group Psychotherapy,* 1956, 9, 89-114.

The uses of roleplaying in personnel and guidance include: 1. improving interpersonal and intercultural relations; 2. changing attitudes and behavior; 3. stimulating group participation, involvement in training, and interest in academic subjects; 4. developing spontaneity; 5. serving as a technique for personnel selections and situational diagnosis; 6. helping the individual with inner conflicts and problems; 7. aiding research explorations.

62. McDONALD, MARGHERITA A. Psychodrama explores a private world. *Sociatry,* 1947, 1, 97-118.

Miss McDonald discusses a psychodramatic didactic session in which she participated having previously served as a subject in a didactic session with Carl Rogers, using the same problem situation. In comparing the two approaches, she feels that the non-directive method which gives the individual an opportunity to express whatever he feels without receiving approval or disapproval, is unrealistic. The client is limited by the structure of the situation, which permits him to do nothing but just sit and talk about his problem. Psychodrama enables the subject to move within his own framework as he normally does. being creative and realistic.

63. MANN, J. H. Experimental evaluation of roleplaying. *Psychological Bulletin,* 1956, 53, 227-234.

A roleplaying situation occurs when an individual formally assumes a role not normally his own; or if his own, in a setting not normal for the enactment of the role. There is evidence that reliable and valid roleplaying personality assessment tests can be developed. There is as yet little supportive evidence that roleplaying is an effective method for personality change.

64. MANN, J. H. The effect of role playing experience on self-ratings of interpersonal adjustment. *Group Psychotherapy*, 1958, 11, 27-32.

This study investigated the hypothesis that roleplaying experience increases interpersonal adjustment. Subjects in a graduate course in education were randomly assigned to groups of eight and met for one hour four times a week over a period of three weeks. The experimental groups engaged in roleplaying while control groups met in a leaderless group discussion. The difference between groups with respect to self-ratings indicated significantly greater change among role players than among control subjects, thus supporting the hypothesis.

65. MEIERS, J. Scandinavian myth about the psychodrama. A counterstatement to S. R. Slavson's "Preliminary note." *Group Psychotherapy,* 1957, 10, 349-352.

Meiers offers a rebuttal to Slavson's article (see 112) which claimed psychodrama was originated by Karl Joergensen. Meiers contends Slavson arrived at his conclusions on the basis of five lines of an article written by Ernest Harms,* which stated that Joergensen

* Harms, E. "Group Therapy—Farce, Fashion, or Sociologically Sound?" *Nervous Child* (1945), 4, 186-95.

used "dramatic diagnosis and therapy" later imported to America and trademarked as "psychodramatics." Meiers presents statements by Karl Joergensen through personal correspondence in which Joergensen denies being the originator of psychodrama. Joergensen felt the misunderstanding by Harms may have occurred because he related to Harms various dramatic situations which occurred among the patients in the clinic at Hornbaek, where Joergensen was head physician.

66. Moldowsky, S. Sociodrama session at the Mansfield Theater. *Group Psychotherapy*, 1950, 3, 102-105.

This is an account of a psychodramatic session in which the author served as subject. The scene involved his impending marriage and the difficulties he felt he might encounter. He found the audience served as a warm, receptive group which had similar problems. Roleplaying provided him with some insight into his difficulties as well as some practical solutions. The effect on the seven members of the hospital entourage who were present at the session of "baring himself" was that many of them felt the need to give of themselves in conversations. The session seemel to have lifted some barriers in the relationship between the author and these seven members, which precipitated new social experiences. The author feels his ability to direct other people in psychodrama groups is due, in large part, to himself having been a "protagonist."

67. Monod, Mirielle. First French experience with psychodrama. *Sociatry,* 1948, 1, 400-403.

A psychodrama program was inaugurated by the French Child Guidance Clinic of Paris. The subjects consisted of forty-one children referred for various difficulties. Eleven subjects withdrew for various reasons, reducing the final sample to thirty. Weekly sessions were held, with a half hour warm-up period. Subjects were divided into three groups according to age, the age range being nine to seventeen years. The sexes were equally distributed. The criteria of improvement were the staff's impressions during the sessions, the appraisal of the parents which the staff procured by interviews and letters, and finally the impression of the school teacher to whom the staff sent a letter at the end of the school term. Monard concludes the staff attained seventy-three per cent success.

68. MORENO, FLORENCE B. Psychodrama in the neighborhood. *Sociatry,* 1947, 1, 168-178.

A setting for neighborhood groups of children and parents to act out their problems was established at the Psychodramatic Institute at Beacon. Problems which participants have "tried to solve themselves but have failed" are brought to the attention of the director. Mrs. Moreno offers the following comments concerning psychodrama in the neighborhood. Audience reactions are studied by casual remarks, gestures, and facial expressions. Psychodramatic learning must be followed through in actual life situations to become meaningful. Children involved in roleplaying have an opportunity to work out their conflicts without imposed solutions.

69. MORENO, J. L. *Who shall survive?* Washington: Nervous and Mental Disease Publishing Co., 1934, 435 pp.

Moreno summarizes some experimental work concerning the analysis and reconstruction of community and group life. The four main sections of this book are: 1. evolution of groups; 2. the sociometry of groups; 3. the construction and reconstruction of groups; 4. the sociometric planning of society. The analysis is based on the assumption that many individual maladjustments reflect group maladjustments and should be dealt with by adjusting the group relations of the individuals. Tests developed to determine group attitudes on the basis of spontaneity are discussed. Moreno also includes "preludes of the sociometric movement," in which he discusses the genesis of psychodrama, group psychotherapy, sociometry, and related topics.

70. MORENO, J. L. Psychodramatic shock therapy: a sociometric approach to the problem of mental disorders. *Sociometry,* 1939, 2, 1-30.

During lucid intervals of the psychotic attack or immediately after it, the patient can be stimulated by the use of a psychodramatic warming up process to throw himself back into the psychotic world. This upsetting experience is called "psychodramatic shock," which offers a research method for the study of the psychoses and has a cathartic effect upon patients. Psychodramatic shock enhances spontaneity and creates barriers aginst psychotic recurrrence. This approach is illustrated by three case studies of a schizophrenic, a manic-depressive, and a psychoneurotic.

71. MORENO, J. L. Psychodramatic treatment of psychoses. *Sociometry*, 1940, 2, 115-132.

The psychodramatic principle provides for objectification of experiences by means of the establishment of an "imaginary reality." The application of this principle to psychotic patients involves an investigation of the extent to which the patient is able to form an imaginary reality. When this has been determined, the appropriate psychodramatic techniques that can be utilized with psychotic patients are: 1. mirror technique; 2. projective technique; 3. role reversal; 4. symbolic distance; 5. double ego techniques; 6. auxiliary world technique. Reports of thirty-three psychotic patients treated by these psychodramatic techniques are given.

72. MORENO, J. L. *Psychodrama: Volume I.* New York: Beacon House, 1946, 429 pp.

The first of three volumes concerning the technique of psychodrama contains psychodramatic protocols and documents outlining the development of psychodrama. The nine sections include: 1. the cradle of psychodrama; 2. the therapeutic theatre; 3. creative revolutions; 4. principles of spontaneity; 5. role theory and role practice; 6. psychodrama; 7. psychomusic; 8. sociodrama; 9. therapeutic motion pictures.

73. MORENO, J. L. Psychodrama of a pre-marital couple. (A protocol.) *Sociatry*, 1947, 2, 103-120.

Moreno presents a protocol of a session involving an engaged couple illustrating the self-directed form of psychodrama in which subjects initiate practically all ideas and actions. The effect of the session was threefold: 1. as a diagnostic test; 2. as a prophylactic measure; 3. as a didactic procedure, teaching prematrimonial and matrimonial behavior to university students who were spectators.

74. MORENO, J. L. Hypnodrama and psychodrama. *Group Psychotherapy,* 1950, 3, 1-10.

Moreno divides psychiatry into three categories: confessional (psychoanalysis), Shakespearian (psychodrama), and Machiavellian (electric shock, insulin shock and lobotomy). Psychodrama brings the three efforts into a synthesis. Hypnodrama is a synthesis of psychodrama and hypnosis.

75. MORENO, J. L. Fragments from the psychodrama of a dream. *Group Psychotherapy,* 1951, 3, 344-365.

In psychodramatic dream therapy, subjects with recurring dreams reproduce the dream on the stage and are then urged to extend its limits for a better understanding and control. They learn to apply this technique to other dreams on a deep action level, thus becoming their own dream therapist.

76. MORENO, J. L. Sociodramatic approach to minority problems. *Group Psychotherapy,* 1952, 5, 7-19.

A protocol in which the sociodramatic approach was used to deal with minority problems is presented. An historical account of sociodrama is provided as well as differentiating it from psychodrama. Role structures of a group, role categories, and some roleplaying techniques, such as role reversal are stressed. An important reason for determining role relations, through sociodrama, is its value as a guide for further investigation and treatment.

77. MORENO, J. L. Sociodrama of a family conflict. *Group Psychotherapy,* 1952, 5, 20-37.

A transcript is presented of a session illustrating the combining of the solution of social problems with personality study. Moreno set up the following roles to be portrayed by group members in various scenes: 1. the role of authority, as the father toward his child, son or daughter; 2. the role of the supported father;

3. the role of the paternal lover. When a situation is not completely structured, the subjects project something of their own as they warm up to the situation.

78. MORENO, J. L. Psychodramatic production techniques. *Group Psychotherapy,* 1952, 4, 243-273.

The double techniques, the mirror technique, and the reversal technique can be compared to three stages of development of the infant: 1. the stage of identity (double); 2. the stage of the recognition of the self (mirror); 3. stage of the recognition of the other (reversal). A transcript of a psychodrama session illustrates the three techniques.

79. MORENO, J. L. The discovery of the spontaneous man with special emphasis upon the technique of role reversal. *Group Psychotherapy,* 1955, 8, 103-129.

A description of the methodology and technique of role reversal in its special application to infants and children is offered. In role reversal, the subject learns how to function in an unusual role. It can be applied to a number of situations such as: a correction for general rebelliousness; a three-way role reversal between father, mother, and child; and treatment of temper tantrums. Illustrations are given for these situations. Twenty-six hypotheses concerning the use of role reversal with infants and children are given.

80. MORENO, J. L. Psychodrama. In S. Arieti (Ed.), *American Handbook of Psychiatry.* Vol. II. New York: Basic Books, Inc., 1959. Pp. 1357-1396.

Moreno provides an historical background, origins, and the fundamental rules of psychodrama. A detailed account of the various psychodramatic techniques is offered as well as the many modifications of the psychodramatic method.

81. MORENO, J. L. Role theory and the emergence of the self. *Group Psychotherapy,* 1962, 15, 114-117.

Roleplaying is prior to the emergence of the self. Roles do not emerge from the self, but the self emerges from roles. The first roles to emerge are the physiological or psychosomatic roles. They help the infant experience what we call the "body." This is followed by the development of psychodramatic roles and transactions, which help the infant to experience the "psyche." Finally, the social roles develop to produce "society." Body, psyche, and society are then the intermediary parts of the entire self.

82. MORENO, J. L. The third psychiatric revolution and the scope of psychodrama. *Group Psychotherapy,* 1964, 17, 149-171.

Moreno contends that changes brought about by the first psychiatric revolution (Pinel), were institutional and those brought about by the second (Freud), were psychodynamic. The third revolution signaled by the advent of group and action methods, has as its ultimate goal a therapeutic society, a therapeutic world order. Moreno discusses creativity, spontaneity, the universe as a frame of reference, telic sensitivity and co-unconscious states and the "inter-psyche." He presents eight hypotheses concerning his views on the need for mass psychiatry.

83. MORENO, J. L. Psychodrama in action. *Group Psychotherapy,* 1965, 18, 87-117.

Moreno presents a text abstracted from a televised motion picture made at a large mental hospital in the U.S.A. Moreno was the director of a group of patients and the scene was communicated via closed circuit television to several thousand patients in the various wards of the hospital. The problem concerned the readiness of patients for discharge. The psychodramatic exit test, a method to determine the patient's readiness for returning to the community, was the primary technique used.

84. MORENO, ZERKA. Psychodrama in a well-baby clinic. *Group Psychotherapy,* 1951, 4, 100-106.

The problems of mothers with newborn children can be dealt with through role-reversal. The psychodramatist takes the role of the infant to provide insight into the feelings of a newborn baby. This stimulates mothers through a triple feeling—what kind of mothers they are, how they perceive their babies, and in what type of milieu they function.

85. MORENO, ZERKA. A survey of psychodramatic techniques. *Group Psychotherapy,* 1959, 12, 5-14.

A discussion of the following techniques is presented: 1. soliloquy; 2. therapeutic soliloquy; 3. self-presentation; 4. hallucinatory psychodrama; 5. double; 6. multiple double; 7. mirror; 8. dream; 9. symbolic realization. 10. analytic psychodrama; 11. auxiliary world; 12. treatment at a distance; 13. warming up; 14. spontaneous improvisations; 15. mirror-behind your back—a) behind your back audience, b) turn your back, c) black out; 16. magic shop.

86. MORENO, ZERKA. Psychodramatic rules, techniques and adjunctive methods. *Group Psychotherapy,* 1965, 18, 73-86.

Fifteen basic rules of psychodrama are presented, which provide the method's rationale as well as sequential guidelines for the practitioner. Moreno defines some of the more widely used psychodramatic techniques and briefly discusses adjunctive methods, such as hypnodrama, didactic psychodrama and roleplaying, psychodramatic shock, improvisation of personality assessment, psychodrama combined with narcosynthesis, and family therapy.

87. NICHOLS, FLORENCE L. Psychiatrist and nurse as co-therapists in a psychodrama group. *Group Psychotherapy,* 1962, 15, 197-199.

Psychodrama was conducted with a group of eighteen adults, mostly married couples. The therapists alternated as director, and as auxiliary ego. Some of the couples, became more frank in communicating with each other. Group members communicated between sessions, especially giving support to the last session's protagonist. The psychodrama sessions facilitated the individual sessions.

88. O'CONNELL, W. E. Adlerian psychodrama with schizophrenics. *Journal of Individual Psychology,* 1963, 19, 69-76.

O'Connell's psychodramatic methods were originally based on Moreno's views; however, he now leans toward the Adlerian approach. This shift in viewpoint is due to relatively greater ease in communicating Adlerian premises which make sense in treating schizophrenia.

89. OSSORIO, A. G. & FINE, L. Psychodrama as a catalyst for social change in a mental hospital. *Progress in Psychotherapy,* 1960, 5, 122-131.

Ossorio and Fine developed procedures intended to facilitate change in hospital ward of seventy-three female patients primarily diagnosed as chronic schizophrenic. Psychodramatic methods were selected because of their potentiality for influencing simultaneously both growth and individual processes. Psychodrama involved both staff and patients in an emotionally re-educative experience. In general, the authors felt psychodramatic methods provide maximum entry into the world of the patient. Various techniques were used, including *amplification,* in which the therapist repeats aloud words or actions of the patient so that they can be shared by all participants. The authors conclude that the overall ward attitude became much less pessimistic and the patients became more aware of themselves and their environment.

90. PARRISH, MARGUERITE. The development of a psychodrama program in a state hospital setting. *Group Psychotherapy,* 1958, 11, 63-68.

Factors to consider when establishing a psychodrama program in a state hospital are: 1. amount of personnel and space available; 2. personality of the director; 3. training of auxiliary egos; 4. general orientation to the staff and patients; 5. selection and casting of patients; 6. goals of the group. Psychodrama can be used anywhere; the one essential prerequisite is that the director have sufficient training to handle the proposed level of treatment.

91. Parrish, Marguerite. The effect of short term psychodrama on chronic schizophrenic patients. *Group Psychotherapy,* 1959, 12, 15-26.

Psychodrama was employed with thirty-seven women diagnosed as chronic schizophrenics. Psychologically oriented movies helped establish group feeling and served as a springboard for dramatization. The scenes ranged from portrayals of husband-wife relationships to feelings about the hospital or about leaving the hospital. No control group was used to determine what could be attributed solely to the effects of psychodrama, but a majority showed marked improvement in socialization. Psychodrama is useful with this type of patient because roleplaying facilitates verbalization, and affects the unrealistic thinking of the psychotic patient.

92. Parrish, Marguerite. Group techniques with teen-age emotionally disturbed girls. *Group Psychotherapy,* 1961, 14, 20-25.

Group procedures were used with a group of adolescent girls for whom individual treatment had either failed or been of limited value. In the group sessions, underlying problems were uncovered and were then followed by therapeutic roleplaying. Members were encouraged to act out personal problems. While the group experience did not cure these girls, it succeeded in drastically altering attitudes toward authority as well as changing their self-image and their image of their families.

93. Parrish, Marguerite & Mitchell, J. Psychodrama in Pontiac State Hospital. *Group Psychotherapy,* 1951, 4, 80-84.

Seventy-nine patients, the majority diagnosed as schizophrenic, were subjects in psychodrama. Sessions helped patients: 1. by resocializing them in a friendly, accepting group; 2. by re-establishing interpersonal relationships; 3. by satisfying emotional needs and diminishing anxiety; 4. by the feeling of success deriving from overcoming imaginary problem situations before a group of one's peers and by knowledge and acquired "know-how" from trial and error explorations; 5. by developing self-awareness through reality testing experiences. The results indicate only ten out of the seventy-seven patients manifested little or no evidence of improvement following participation.

94. PILKEY, LORAINE, GOLDMAN, M. & KLEINMAN, B. Psychodrama and empathetic ability in the mentally retarded. *American Journal of Mental Deficiency,* 1961, 65, 595-605.

Two groups of sixteen eighth-grade mentally retarded boys and girls were used to test whether the empathetic ability of the mentally retarded adolescent could be improved through psychodramatic training as evidenced by greater accuracy in the ability to predict certain responses of others. The experiment lasted four weeks, the experimental group receiving two one-hour psychodrama training sessions each week. Subjects made ratings of themselves and predicted the self-ratings of five other children in their class at the beginning and end of the study, as well as six weeks after the training had ended. The hypothesis was partially supported, with improvement in the prediction of some traits in others changing significantly for those who received psychodramatic training.

95. POTTS, F. Relief of an anxiety state by a single psychodramatic session. *Group Psychotherapy,* 1958, 11, 331-332.

The case of a thirty-two year old woman having marital difficulties and psychosomatic symptoms is presented. She was seen in individual and group therapy with little success, at which time her therapist decided to try psychodrama, through which she was able to express feelings causing her anxiety. At the next group meeting, she reported a reduction of anxiety and of symptoms. Potts concludes remission is based on: 1. the cathartic power of spontaneity per se; 2. normal re-channelizing of disturbed emotions through dramatization and acting out; 3. multiple roles assumed by the patient which permitted her to introject her problems as a totality; 4. help and support given her by the complex phenomena of tele-transference relation to therapist and auxiliary, egos.

96. RACKOW, L. L. Modified insulin, psychodrama, and rehabilitation techniques in the treatment of anxiety and tension states. *Group Psychotherapy,* 1951, 4, 215-222.

The method of treatment involving modified insulin combined with psychodrama is discussed with the results in a series of ninety-eight cases. Recurrence of the anxiety and tension was reported by eighty-five percent of those who initially benefited from the above treatment within a relatively short time. Patients in the group were more easily accessible and partook more freely in the psychodrama sessions than a similar group of patients who were treated previously by psychodrama without insulin therapy. Psychodrama sessions were conducted immediately following the insulin therapy. The different approaches to acting out the psychodynamics or the experience situations appeared to be beneficial to the group as a whole. On some occasions, abreactions were noted in the principal actors, but the main benefit of the experience appeared to be in the sphere of insight and experience gaining. This method did not produce permanent results, relapse occurring in a large percentage of the cases when they returned to the stresses and strains of everyday life.

97. RIESSMAN, F. Role-playing and the lower socio-economic group. *Group Psychotherapy,* 1964, 17, 36-48.

Four reasons why roleplaying is valuable with low income groups are: 1. it is congenial with the low income person's style: physical (do vs. talk); 2. the professional worker reduces role distance between himself and the disadvantaged person; 3. it changes the setting and tone of what often appears to the low-income person as an office-ridden, impersonal, foreign procedure; 4. it facilitates verbalization in the educationally deprived person. Professional people are often resistant to roleplaying because they fear what they believe to be its sensationalistic, charlatanlike overtones. Riessman offers the following suggestions to overcome some of these resistances: 1. artificial elements be sharply reduced; 2. simple language be used to refer to roleplaying technology; 3. roleplaying techniques be combined with other techniques; 4. the psychotherapeutic functions of roleplaying be made explicit; 5. specific uses of roleplaying be carefully elaborated and exemplified in great detail both didactically and by illustration; 6. it be made clear that roleplaying is not necessarily tied to any particular theoretic or treatment system; 7. research evidence supporting the value of roleplaying be supplied.

98. ROTHAUS, P. Instrumented role playing in psychiatric training laboratory. *Archives of General Psychiatry,* 1964, 11(4), 400-410.

Instrumented role playing (IRP) consists of the following: 1. roleplaying exercises are formulated as experiments in which the role variations of the participants (patients) constitute the experimental variable. The participants are considered scientists experimenting with the consequences of their own behavior through roleplaying; 2. role variations are determined by a conceptual model; 3. tasks are selected in which roleplaying interaction can take place; 4. practice training in the roles is given. Under optimum conditions, all participants learn to play all role variations; 5. naive subjects, those who react to the roleplaying, and who are not aware that their task partners are roleplaying, are needed for the experiment; 6. these naive subjects rate their task partner's behavior on various scales. These ratings constitute the response variables in the roleplaying experiment; 7. feedback of naive subjects' reactions is given to participants; 8. participants are to discuss and formulate a conceptual theory explaining the data. An illustrative experiment using instrumented roleplaying with twenty-four psychiatric patients is provided. Rothaus concludes that the IRP technique overcomes a great deal of the resistance one often finds to roleplaying. For instance, IRP avoids singling out individuals for specific roles which may make them uncomfortable, and calls for large numbers of subjects to play identical roles simultaneously. Also, with IRP, the subject plays several roles rather than just one specific role, thus reducing the threat of having to make a sweeping change in his behavior pattern and allowing him to choose what changes in his behavior style seem most appropriate. Finally, IRP can make the patient feel as though he is a scientist or learner when roleplaying rather than a sick person demonstrating his ability to change sick behavior.

99. ROTHMAN, GERTRUDE. Psychodrama and autogenic relaxation. *Group Psychotherapy,* 1961, 14, 26-29.

Autogenic training, in a modified form was used in combination with psychodrama, not to lead to deep trance, hypnosis or sleep, but as a relaxant, facilitating the utilization of the psychodrama techniques.

100. ROUTH, T. A. Psychodrama and the blind. *Group Psychotherapy,* 1958, 11, 213-216.

Roleplaying was used to observe reactions of blind persons in rehabilitation centers. The client is encouraged to act out his feelings, attitudes, and emotions with reference to problem areas such as: 1. self-concept; 2. feelings of inadequacy. The content of roleplaying sessions provides topics to be discussed in group lectures and individual therapy. Psychodrama is a prime tool to employ with blind people.

101. RUDHYAR, EVA & BRANHAM, B. The development of a psychodrama department in a mental hospital. *Group Psychotherapy,* 1953, 6, 110-114.

The authors present the mechanics of developing a psychodrama department in a State Mental Institute. Open group sessions are held for outside visistors, various employees, and patients, the purpose being to provide the experience of how a "democratic" group functions. The two psychodramatists provided individual therapy to approximately ten members of the regular groups, utilizing the psychodramatic interview and action techniques. The two therapists observed each other in action to maintain a high level of consistency. The authors feel that mental hospitals may eventually become re-education centers in their communities, with an orientation toward group psychotherapy and psychodrama.

102. SACKS, J. M. The judgment technique in psychodrama. *Group Psychotherapy,* 1965, 18, 69-72.

Sacks describes a psychodrama scene in which the protagonist is encouraged to explore judgmental situations by role reversal. This is usually done by placing the protagonist in the role of the judgmental figures in his life or by the use of partially hypothetical situations such as courtroom scenes. This technique assists the therapist in dealing with the defendant-judge relationship that may exist in therapy.

103. SARBIN, T. R. Spontaneity training of the feebleminded. *Sociatry,* 1945, 7, 389-393.

Roleplaying seems to be an ideal procedure for evaluating and training mental defectives. The degree of competence held at present as well as potential can be estimated by these action techniques. As a method of improvement, spontaneity exercises are both meaningful and practical, not only for the participant but also for the observers in a group setting in an institution for the feebleminded.

104. SARBIN, T. R. Role theory. In G. Lindzey (Ed.), *Handbook of social psychology.* Vol. I, 1954, Pp. 223-258.

Role theory attempts to conceptualize human conduct at a relatively complex level. Its variables are drawn from studies of culture, society, and personality. The broad conceptual units of the theory are: 1. role, the unit of culture; 2. position, the unit of society; 3. self, the unit of personality. Persons occupy positions or status in interactional situations. Positions are cognitive systems of role expectations, products of learning. Role expectations are bidimensional; for every role expectation of others there is a reciprocal role expectation of self. The organized actions of the person, directed toward fulfilling these role expectations, comprise the role. Variation in role enactment is a function of at least three variables: 1. the validity of role perception (this implies the concurrent or just-prior perception and locating of the position of other and reciprocally of self); 2. skill in role enactment (related to practice in the use of "as if" behavior); 3. the current organization of the self—a cognitive structure that exercises a selective and directive effect on role perception and role enactment. Sarbin reviews some experiments which have emerged from role theory as well as empirical methods available for assessing the self.

105. SCHAUER, G. The function of an audience analyst in psychodrama. *Group Psychotherapy,* 1951, 4, 197-205.

The audience analyst critically interprets therapeutic sessions to introduce the audience's point of view. The problems of the spectator can be dealt with in group psychodrama, while directive psychoanalytic and non-directive methods fall short in meeting the needs of many patients.

106. SCHER, J. M. Two disruptions of the communication zone: a discussion of action and role playing techniques. *Group Psychotherapy,* 1959, 12, 127-133.

Communicata retarda, occurs when communication lacks true goal-intendedness. *Communicata multiplex,* occurs when too much information is fed into the system or too many unorganized or competing channels are receiving communications simultaneously or serially. One method of achieving correction is to employ role-playing to clarify the situation and to lead to meaningful decision taking.

107. SHELLOW, R. Psychodramatic and group psychotherapy. *Group Psychotherapy,* 1958, 11, 227-228.

Inmates of a juvenile institution tend to be non-introspective and usually "act out" problem solutions. When properly utilized, this "acting out" can be turned to therapeutic advantage. An example of the spontaneous eruption of latent group problems into dramatic form is described.

108. SHOOBS, N. E. Individual psychology and psychodrama. *American Journal of Individual Psychology,* 1956, 12, 46-52.

Therapists with an Adlerian orientation can utilize psychodramatic techniques without adhering to the philosophy of J. L. Moreno.

109. SHOOBS, N. E. Role-playing in the individual psychotherapy interview. *Journal of Individual Psychology,* 1964, 20, 84-89.

Shoobs reports incidents in which he used role-playing, with resisting, noncooperative individuals, employing different variations in individual psychotherapy. With a patient having difficulty making a decision, the *double technique* was used. Shoobs used *role-reversal* to overcome a patient's inadequacy feelings. To deal with resistance, Shoobs used *role-exchange* with the patient. Illustrations are provided of the *soliloquy technique* and *trait personifications.* In visiodrama, Shoobs makes use of cartoons and drawings to warm up resistive patients for actual roleplaying. These methods provide patients with opportunities for practicing social skills, for meeting difficult situations, and for taking responsibilities, helping them to gain insight and be more aware of others.

110. SHOR, J. A modified psychodrama technique for rehabilitation of military psychoneurotics. *Sociatry,* 1948, 1, 414-420.

The psychodrama "integrator" in a military hospital interviews patients explaining that dramatic activity is part of the treatment program. During the interview, patients are asked to discuss post discharge plans, with emphasis on situations which patients feel might cause difficulty upon discharge. The integrator gave auxiliary egos information about the patients and the planned program for the day. Each session was concluded with an open conference between patient and integrator. Subsequently, the session was reported to the ward doctor by the integrator. Anxiety neurotic patients showed the most complete emotional involvement and an increase in self-insight. Organically brain injured patients simply reiterated preoccupations and sense of impotency, failing to respond well to psychodrama. Schizophrenics could not warm up and usually refused to accept any externally suggested fantasy situation.

111. SHULMAN, B. H. A psychodramatically oriented action technique in group psychotherapy. *Group Psychotherapy,* 1960, 13, 34-39.

The members of a therapeutic group tried to discover the hidden purpose of a member's provocative behavior and then in an exaggerated way, responded to the behavior. This conveyed to the patient his intentions dramatically and forcefully. Confrontation of one's mistaken goals via others' roleplaying responses often leads to an immediate release of tension and correction of behavior.

112. SLAVSON, S. R. A preliminary note on the relation of psychodrama and group psychotherapy. *International Journal of Group Psychotherapy,* 1955, 5, 361-366.

Slavson states that psychodrama was originated by Karl Joergensen of Sweden who introduced the spontaneity theater, or *Stegrief theatre* in 1915 which was later transplanted to the United States by J. L. Moreno. Slavson maintains that spontaneity techniques can be usefully employed as a "catharsis inducer," a rehearsal technique, and a means of communication, but never as total therapy. The psychodramatic technique may be used with psychotics to activate communication; however, for nonpsychotic patients, roleplaying and other psychodramatic methods are artificial. Slavson concludes that psychodrama must be used with discrimination with patients for which it is suitable. Blanket use of psychodrama is not only wasteful, but is definitely injurious and confusing. (Also see Abstract No. 65.)

113. SMIGEL, E. O. A note on audience involvement and roleplaying in sociodrama. *Group Psychotherapy,* 1961, 14, 66-67.

Heightened involvement of the audience occurs when the audience is told they will be called upon to criticize, add to, discuss, or give their own version of how the roles should have been played. With this technique the audience becomes more attentive; the actors, because of possible criticism, tend to take their parts more seriously; and additional insights occur to the group.

114. SMITH, MARION REED. The "silent" auxiliary-ego technique in rehabilitating deteriorated mental patients. *Group Psychotherapy,* 1950, 3, 92-100.

Seventeen deteriorated psychiatric patients hospitalized an average of sixteen years, were studied in a group habit-training project. The "silent auxiliary-ego" technique, in which activities are suggested by gesture rather than speech, was used. Some goals of the project, as demonstrated in four case studies were: 1. bringing back mental vitality; 2. presenting occupations likely to appeal; 3. helping an uncooperative patient; 4. finding projects that suited the patient's ability and whim. Results were generally positive. Ward attendants' interest in helping patients increased by introducing a new method of approaching the patients.

115. SOLOMON, A. P. & FENTRESS, T. L. A critical study of analytically oriented group psychotherapy utilizing the technique of dramatization of the psychodynamics. *Occupational Therapy and Rehabilitation,* 1947, 26, 23-46.

Dramatization of the patient's pspchodynamics is an effective method in conjunction with group psychotherapy for 1. obtaining abreactions; 2. increasing insight into unconscious material; and 3. modifying overly rigid, strict super-egos or strengthening weak super-egos. A study of thirty-four patients and fifty-five dramatizations indicates that it is possible to obtain strong abreaction in all of the categories studied except for compulsive neurotics and schizoids. Strong tension during the writing of an autobiography is associated with weak abreaction in dramatization. The dramatization technique is felt to be effective as a teaching method in the group therapy of the patients in the audience by diminishing restistance, increasing insight, and permitting abreactions by identification.

116. SPIEGEL, J. P. Psychotherapy as a system of social roles. *Journal of Nervous and Mental Diseases*, 1954, 120, 395.

Roles have structural and functional aspects. The structural aspects can be classified as goal, value, and allocative. The functional aspects of roles arise out of the degree of goodness of fit or strain in their structural aspects. Role reversal is defined as an emergency attempt to restore complimentarity by taking a role opposite to that which one has been playing. Explicit and implicit roles are discussed.

117. STARR, ADALINE. Psychodrama with a child's social atom. *Group Psychotherapy*, 1953, 5, 222-225.

The child's social atom includes all who people his life situation. As the child grows, more roles are added to his behavior repertoire. In psychodrama with children the director's goal is not interpretation dynamics, but expression. When too much anxiety is exhibited the acting can be directed by the child. The group may act out dreams, day-dreams, or experiences as related by the child. A problem in doing private practice group psychotherapy with children, is the difficulty in forming a group which will afford the child with a maximum of satisfaction in positive relationships. Family psychodrama affords an opportunity for recreating life situations, giving the child and family a chance to go back to repeat experiences as they would prefer to have done them, or to attempt entirely new approaches. Family members can be trained to be therapeutic agents to each other, not at the intellectual level, but in the action process.

118. STEIN, C. Psychodrama for nurses in a general hospital. *Group Psychotherapy*, 1961, 14, 90-94.

Weekly psychodrama sessions for student and registered nurses helped to resolve emotional tensions connected with hospital duties. The nurses became more aware of their feelings and became better equipped to deal with hospital situations as well as their own personal and family lives. An effective way of replacing a sense of failure with an ego-lifting experience is to reverse roles, or to put the nurse into an authoritarian or therapeutic role so that she can attain a feeling of accomplishment.

119. STEINMETZ, MARTHA A. An experiment in psychodrama at the Florence Crittenden Maternity Home. *Group Psychotherapy,* 1958, 11, 216-218.

Roleplaying was used with unmarried girls residing in a maternity home: 1. to help them gain insight into their problems and to help them work out methods of approaching their family and friends; 2. to evolve adjustment techniques pertinent to a homogeneous and structured environment. A combination of group discussion, along with roleplaying, was found most helpful.

120. STEVENS, ELISABETH. Psychodrama in the speech clinic. *Sociatry,* 1947, 1, 56-58.

To the extent that speech difficulties are not due to somatic defects, they represent symptoms of personality maladjustment. Usual verbal techniques place limitations on therapeutic progress because of patient's difficulty in communicating. The psychodramatic method because of its deemphasis of verbal communication has advantages in the treatment of speech defective patients because of their ability to show conflicts on a non-verbal level.

121. STREAN, H. S. Treating parents of emotionally disturbed children through role playing. *Psychoanalysis and Psychoanalytic Review,* 1960, 47 (1) 67-76.

Roleplaying may be used with the severely disturbed parent who has strong resistance to change, limited ego functions, and whose psychic balance depend on a pathological parent-child relationship. Through roleplaying, the therapist provides the parent-patient with a new symbolic parent to be introjected as a corrective emotional experience. The role played by the therapist is influenced by his evaluation of the parent's childhood experiences with his own parents.

122. STURM, I. E. The behavioristic aspects of psychodrama. *Group Psychotherapy,* 1965, 18, 50-64.

Sturm recognizes the differences in the philosophical basis and goals between the psychodrama and psychodramatic group psychotherapy system and the learning theory and behavior therapy system. In an attempt to combine the methods, Sturm describes six basic psychodramatic techniqes from within the behavior therapy framework and six prominent behavior therapy techniques are reviewed from within a psychodramatic emphasis. Sturm offers a synthesis of the two systems, which he labels "behavioristic psychodrama" and hypothesizes that this synthesis will provide a useful repertoire of behavioral control techniques.

123. TAWADROS, S. M. Spontaneity training at the Dorra Institute, Alexandria, Egypt. *Group Psychotherapy,* 1956, 9, 164-167.

Tawadros designed an experiment which attempted to explore the hypothesis that "morons can be stimulated to react intelligently to social situations through the use of the psychodramatic and spontaneity training methods." Spontaneity training was initially used for the following purposes: 1. analysis of everyday life situations; 2. familiarizing children with the roles of state officials and various trades and professions in the community; 3. generally promoting the children's creative abilities. The children acted out such scenes as a street accident between a bicycle and automobile, choosing their roles and eventually exchanging roles. Tawadros concludes that the results support Sarbins's position as to the value of spontaneity training for feeble-minded children and the author further suggests the psychodrama would be beneficial to these children in reenacting family situation scenes. Psychodrama also was found to be a valuable diagnostic tool with feeble-minded children.

124. TOEMAN, ZERKA. The "double situation" in psychodrama. *Sociatry,* 1948, 1, 436-446.

A subject is given three-dimensional reality when the double and subject perform the same act, thinking and acting in unison. The stimulus comes from the body image of the double and has a profound effect in producing in the subject the image of a co-existing body and mind. When this relationship has been established, the auxiliary ego playing the double role can begin to deviate to stimulate the subject along a different track.

125. TWITCHELL-ALLEN, DORIS. The essence of psychodrama. *Group Psychotherapy,* 1960, 13, 188-194.

Psychodrama is a way of life. It is always available for use in any situation, in any place, with any person. Psychodramatic techniques were employed at Children's International Summer Village, whose program brings individuals of varying nationalities together for close daily living. Psychodrama is especially valuable in situations made more difficult by differences of cultural values.

126. VERVEN, N., WALDFOGEL, S., & YOUNG, R. A. Modified psychodrama and group therapy in a treatment camp. *International Journal of Group Psychotherapy,* 1956, 6, 291-299.

Psychodrama produced a genuine catharsis and led to some insight when used as the primary technique at a camp for emotionally disturbed children. The authors felt that it was more effective in the camp setting than conventional group psychotherapy. The apparent reasons were: 1. psychodrama produced less intensive and complicated transference reactions; 2. it was followed by less regressive acting out in other places in the camp program; 3. because of its make-believe quality, it protected the actors from the anxiety that revelation of distressful emotions creates in other therapeutic situations. In general, psychodrama seemed to be helpful in reducing group tensions and diminishing anxieties stemming from the daily crises of camp living. Problems encountered in developing a therapeutic program at this type of camp are discussed.

127. WEINER, HANNAH. A note on role-playing research. *Group Psychotherapy,* 1959, 12, 67-68.

Fifteen married couples were given a questionnaire requesting personal data and presenting eight roleplaying situations to be solved by writing out answers. The couples were separated into three five-couple groups and each couple enacted one of the situations chosen at random. Participants' performances were rated by group members, the actor's mate, and an expert non-participating observer. Ratings were compared to the answers of the written questionnaire to determine how close the individual couples could accurately predict their behavior.

128. WEINER, HANNAH B. Treating the alcoholic with psychodrama. *Group Psychotherapy,* 1965, 18, 27-49.

Weiner presents interpretations of results she has obtained in treating 300 alcoholics over a four-year period through psychodrama. She feels psychodrama is successful in the treatment of the alcoholic because this methodology demands immersion of the total person-mind, personality, body-into contact with reality in a spontaneous action wherein the individual is in contact with his unconscious, developing skills through ridding himself of himself in practicalness and concreteness without "thinking" but in terms of self-forgetfulness and action. The learning process accrues itself to the individual not by being shown by an authority but by enabling the alcoholic to "get the feel" of the spontaneous way of life through adapting and developing his individual peculiarities. He develops a new sense of accurate alertness of all the senses; perception and action become one, independent of a conscious purpose. He develops a spontaneity close to that of the growing child. Past uses of psychodrama in the treatment and management of alcoholism are discussed.

129. WELLS, CECILIA G. Psychodrama with children in a sociometrically structured setting. *Group Psychotherapy,* 1961, 14, 160-163.

Seven fifth graders participated in six workshops involving roleplaying, sociodrama, and psychodrama with adult participants who were the workshop members. The mutually shared benefits were exciting and rewarding to the children as well as to the workshop members. This was a "truly human adventure in group dynamics," where people of all ages could be themselves more freely, could inter-relate, gain personal insight, and see and feel another's point of view.

130. Wells, Cecilia G. Psychodrama and creative counseling in the elementary school. *Group Psychotherapy*, 1962, 15, 244-252.

Wells uses psychodramatic techniques in handling problems of elementary school children. Illustrations are given of using psychodrama "on the spot," for enactment of future roles, and for dealing with day-to-day and face-to-face situations. Insight seems to follow action and feeling. Psychodramatic techniques provide a heightened awareness of human roles and their significance for education.

131. Wyss, Dieter. *Die psychotherapeutische Behandlung einer Halluzinatorisch-Paranoiden Schizophrnie.* (Psychotherapeutic treatment of a hallucinatory-paranoid schizophrenic.) *Nervenarzt*, 1958, 29, 249-255.

A thirty-year-old patient had been psychotic for several years and had been treated with electroshock and insulin-shock. After an attempt at regular psychoanalysis the author began treatment by psychodrama, i.e., he and his colleagues enacted the delusional and hallucinatory persons and experiences of the patient, gradually improving on his reality-testing. The patient's symptoms were reduced and he attained a better degree of social adjustment.

132. Yablonsky, L. Preparing parolees for essential social roles. *Group Psychotherapy*, 1955, 8, 38-40.

Although the fear and anxiety of parolees and mental patients may be rooted in more complex psychological dynamics, it is necessary that they be prepared to act effectively in key areas in social life. Roleplaying can often cut through the complexity of personality problems and help prepare individuals for these situations. The author's roleplaying procedure consisted of four steps: 1. select key situations and roles; 2. project subject into the situations, using role reversal, double, and other psychodramatic techniques which seem indicated; 3. follow up subject on his performance in actual situations; 4. use roleplaying procedures to have the subject explore other situations and to reinforce his positive actions. Yablonsky offers the following conclusions: 1. there are certain cultural key roles and situations which are difficult. This is especially true of individuals who have been institutionalized. 2. Role-playing can enable the individual to remain in the open community. 3. Acting these various roles gives the subject an opportunity to receive therapeutic benefits from "normal" interaction conditions. 4. Role training allows individuals to experience the correct method of handling "key" roles and situations.

133. ZACHER, A. N. The use of psychodrama in pastoral therapy. *Group Psychotherapy*, 1961, 14, 164-168.

Psychodramatic insights and techniques have a broad application in the church. Role reversal can be used when a person has an unrealistic view of the clergy. Roleplaying can be useful in helping individuals understand themselves better, become more effective in their relations with others, and help them understand, at a deeper level, the social issues of our time. The church is a place where people live together, hence, psychodrama is valuable in this setting.

Glossary

Alter ego. A therapist's assistant who assumes the role of the "inner self" of the protagonist.

Analytic psychodrama. An hypothesis tested on stage to verify its validity. The analyst sits in the audience and observes. Analysis of the material is made immediately after the scene.

Antagonist. An individual who interacts against the protagonist in any roleplaying situation.

Assistant. The therapist's helper who represents absentee persons in the life space of the protagonist or hero of the drama; the auxiliary ego.

Audience analyst. A member of a group who critically interprets the session as a spectator, introducing the audience's point of view.

Audience reaction. A group member shares a problem or experience with the group. He then retires psychologically from the group. He may go behind the screen or turn his back on the other members. The group members discuss the situation and his behavior as honestly and sincerely as they are able. *Also see Behind-the-back.*

Auxiliary chair technique. A method for providing inanimate role players without the embarrassment that assistants may cause shy or inhibited patients. One points out that a chair has legs, arms, a back, and can be moved about to represent the action of an individual or animal. The director steps behind the chair and provides its conversation.

Auxiliary ego. See *Assistant.*

Axiodrama. Roleplaying in relation to ethics and general values.

Behind-the-back technique. A form of group psychotherapy in which the protagonist retires from the group, with his back to the rest of the members, who discuss him while he is "out of the room" psychologically although in the room physically. See also *Audience reaction.*

Black-out technique. The entire theater is darkened although all actions continue as if there would be full daylight. This is done so that the protagonist may go through a painful experience unobserved, to retain for the protagonist the experience of solitude.

Catharsis. Release of tension and anxiety by emotionally reliving the incidents of the past, especially those that have been repressed, and honestly facing the causes of difficulty.

Communicata retarda. Communication which lacks true goal-intendedness.

Communication multiplex. A situation that occurs when too many channels of information are fed into the system simultaneously or when too many unorganized or competing channels are transmitting communications simultaneously or serially.

Director. The general title of the individual in charge of the production of roleplaying or psychodrama. He usually runs the session, develops the situation, controls interaction by starting and stopping the action, determines the employment of various techniques, and leads discussions. He may be totally unsophisticated in the particular problem of the individuals or groups, and so may serve as a technical director without involving himself in the content. Also known as a leader, therapist, integrator, etc.

Double technique. Assistant is placed side by side with the patient, interacting with the patient "as himself," physically being duplicated in space and assisting him in the assessment of his problems.

Dream technique. Reenactment of a dream. The patient lies down, warming up to the sleep situation. When able to reconstruct the dream, he rises from the bed and represents the dream in action, using assistants to enact the roles of the dream characters.

Emergency psychodrama. The use of varying roleplaying techniques in rapid sequence to prevent the patient from mobilizing his resistance but to enable him to tie up the threads sufficiently to resolve his problem.

"Feeling with" method. After a group views a situation, the audience forms subgroups who try to identify with various characters.

Future projection technique. The protagonist demonstrates how he thinks his future will shape itself. He picks a future point in time and space as well as the people he believes will be involved with him in the situation to enact how life may be for him.

Group psychotherapy. A treatment method in which a number of patients meet with a therapist for the purpose of achieving desired personality changes. The roleplaying technique may be used in group as well as in individual therapy.

Hallucinatory psychodrama. The protagonist puts his delusions and hallucinations to a reality test by acting out his fantasies.

Hypnodrama. Used by the therapist to uncover fertile fields of investigation. As soon as the subject is willing to act, he is brought out of the hypnotic state and asked to continue the episode.

Idiopanima. The perception of another's perception of one's self. It is related to insight and empathy. Insight indicates understanding one's self. Empathy refers to the understanding of another. Idiopanima is one's understanding of another's concept of one's self.

Immediate therapy. A technique in therapeutic roleplaying in which a scene is stopped at the climax and the protagonist is immediately sent out of the sessions.

In situ treatment. Therapy "on the spot."

Lifeboat technique. A member of a group is in a "lifeboat," a series of chairs, say four, and he is to "save" three people from the larger group who "enter the boat" and then the sub-group interacts as though on this boat in mid ocean.

Magic shop technique. The director sets up a "magic shop" on the stage. He, or a group member takes the part of the shopkeeper. The shop is filled with imaginary items, values of a non-physical nature. These are not for sale, but they can be obtained in barter, in exchange for other values to be surrendered by the members of the group, either individually or as a group.

Mirror technique. A roleplaying procedure used after a psychodrama. An assistant, taking the place of and imitating the original protagonist, repeats the scene while the former protagonist looks on and sees "himself" as "in a mirror."

Monodrama. Roleplaying which involves one person who may interact with an imaginary antagonist, or in the split-monodrama may himself take both roles.

Multiple roleplaying. Simultaneous reenactment of the same problem by two or more protagonists and two or more assistants. Usually done for training purposes.

Outsight. The analog of *insight.* This term refers to understanding of the motives of others, to comprehending them in depth. It differs from *empathy,* in that it is more intellectual than emotional, and it differs from *idiopanima,* which refers to A's perception of B's perception of A.

Peak experience. Personal and private experiences of enormous emotional significance which may lead to rapid changes in personality; possibly the causes of conversion experiences.

Protagonist. The "hero" or "chief character" in any roleplaying or psychodrama situation, who contends with or against other individuals known as antagonists.

Psychodrama. Roleplaying by a person of his own past, present or future situation. Often, but incorrectly, equated with roleplaying, the more inclusive term for spontaneity action techniques.

Replaying. Repeating an experience several times to help the subject overcome a traumatic experience. It may also be used to help replace outmoded behavior through the effects of practice.

Roleplaying. Any of several more specific forms of spontaneous action techniques when used for instruction or amelioration of individuals or groups. The essence of roleplaying is "making believe" that the situation is "real"—acting in a spontaneous manner.

Role reversal. An individual exchanges roles with another which facilitates the seeing of the other person's viewpoint. It also makes it possible for the individual who has played one role to move into the other role and demonstrate how he would like to have been treated. If the role reversal takes place during the enactment, this is known as "switching."

Silent auxiliary technique. Actions without speech, which often relax and make certain types of patients more amenable to therapy, such as those with speech defects, certain schizophrenics, and regressed patients.

Simultaneity. An explanation for the strong effects of roleplaying as a learning method: the simultaneous effect of cognitive, emotional and behavioral elements.

Sociodrama. Roleplaying which focuses on the problem of the group. Thus, if a teacher roleplays his problem before students to help them understand him, and if the effect is to enable them to modify their behavior, the treatment is directed to the socius, the group.

Sociometry. A method for measuring the feeling interaction patterns of individuals to other members of any group. It can be depicted by a sociometric map which consists of lines of preferred relationships between individuals. From such sociometric maps one can determine the major individuals in the groups, cliques, isolates, etc.

Soliloquy technique. The subject shares with the group or the director his normally censored feelings and thoughts. The subject turns to one side and expresses his feelings in a voice different from that used in the dialogue.

Spectator therapy. Treatment of an individual which occurs when he observes another, especially in a roleplaying situation.

Spontaneity. The ability to respond adequately to a new situation or to respond in a new and adequate way to an old situation.

Switching. The exchange of roles. Thus when A(B) and C(D) interact, and A and B change roles, to A(D)-C(B) there is a role reversal during the course of the action. In one scene, people may switch roles several times.

Transference. Process whereby a patient shifts feelings applicable to another person onto the psychotherapist, the assistant, or the group. For example, the patient directs upon the therapist the hatred he feels toward his father.

Veridicality. The truthfulness or the subjective reality of roleplaying. If a person becomes angry with his antagonist he has a veridical emotional experience.

Warm up. The process of getting an individual or group to loosen up and become ready to actively participate in the session.

Index

For Product Safety Concerns and Information please contact our EU
representative GPSR@taylorandfrancis.com
Taylor & Francis Verlag GmbH, Kaufingerstraße 24, 80331 München, Germany

www.ingramcontent.com/pod-product-compliance
Ingram Content Group UK Ltd.
Pitfield, Milton Keynes, MK11 3LW, UK
UKHW022025061126
477531UK00002B/29

* 9 7 8 1 1 3 8 5 3 2 0 8 3 *